San Francisco Peninsula Bike Trails

Road and Mountain Bicycle Rides
through San Francisco and San Mateo Counties

by
Conrad J. Boisvert

Penngrove Publications
50 Crest Way
Penngrove, CA 94951
(707) 795-8911

For my mother, Helen

Library of Congress Catalog Card Number 91-61544
International Standard Book Number 0-9621694-3-9

Cover photograph by Jeff Dooley
Taken at Fort Point in San Francisco
Cyclists: Conrad Boisvert and Kathy Picard

Photographs taken by Conrad Boisvert, unless otherwise noted.

Printed in the United States of America

Lithocraft, Inc.
424 Aviation Blvd.
Santa Rosa, California

First printing, November 1991

Penngrove Publications
50 Crest Way
Penngrove, CA 94951
(707) 795-8911

TABLE OF CONTENTS

ACKNOWLEDGMENTS

In expressing my sincere appreciation to the many individuals and organizations who helped me in the preparation of this book, I must begin with my dear mother, whose nurture and support throughout my life has given me the ambition to accomplish more than I ever anticipated. To my wonderful children, Judy, Charles and Steve, I also owe deep gratitude for their encouragement of my efforts.

The many friends who rode endlessly with me, exploring new roads and trails, include Kathy Picard, Dennis Vanata, Sue Johnson, Robert Warman, J. C. Henderson, Pam Silberstein, Richard Wong, Bob Fruehsamer, Beverly Kiltz, Massa Baroudi, and Laurie Nierenberg. Thanks also to Judy Johnson for her encouragement and helpful tips.

The many helpful bike shops throughout the Peninsula never failed to assist me with any questions I had about roads and routes in their vicinity. The rangers and support persons of the various State Parks, County Parks, and Open Space Preserves deserve special note for their knowledge and advice in using the trails.

Special thanks goes to my publisher, Phyllis Neumann, for her many helpful ideas and suggestions, and for her prompt handling of the numerous problems commonly encountered in an undertaking such as this. Jeff Dooley, for his outstanding cover photograph also deserves recognition.

Shoreline Park in Mountain View

EXPLORE THE PENINSULA BY BIKE!

Blessed with a near-perfect climate, a wide variety of terrain, spectacular natural beauty, and close proximity to the Pacific Ocean and San Francisco Bay, the San Francisco Peninsula is a cylist's paradise. Few places can compare with the Peninsula for the wealth of enjoyment and challenge available along the many country roads, all within an hour's drive from nearly any population center.

Stretching from the city of San Francisco in the north to Palo Alto in the south, and from the Bay in the east to the ocean in the west, the Peninsula encompasses flatlands in the Santa Clara Valley, redwood forests in the Santa Cruz Mountain Range, and the rugged coastline so characteristic of Northern California. The large population of the area and the ever-increasing popularity of recreational cycling have combined to fuel the search for the best roads and parks for riding.

Although there are plenty of pleasurable rides available within population centers, such as San Francisco and Palo Alto, the best ones are reached by short trips into the outlying countryside. Traveling along remote rural roads with little or no car traffic, cyclists are rewarded with the true pleasure of the outdoors and with natural scenery as varied as any that can be imagined. The wooded foothills around Woodside and the remote country roads along the coast are examples of the outstanding bike riding experiences accessible on the Peninsula.

Off-road riding is plentiful as well, especially with the recent opening of large amounts of land purchased by the Midpeninsula Regional Open Space District. Open space preserves, although well-supported by trail signs, maps and convenient parking areas, remain relatively undeveloped in order to allow their full enjoyment without disturbing their natural state. Mountain bikers, equestrians, and hikers all share the trails within the preserves. County and State Parks, although more developed, offer spectacular scenic rides through the forests along well-marked trails and often have educational and informative displays at each park headquarters.

The rides in *San Francisco Peninsula Bike Trails* have been selected to appeal to the recreational cyclist. A wide variety of riding levels ensures that sufficient challenge is available, as well, for those wishing to enjoy a more leisurely ride. Don't hesitate — get on your bike and experience the joys of cycling the San Francisco Peninsula.

REGIONS ON THE SAN FRANCISCO PENINSULA

San Francisco and the Upper Peninsula

The upper end of the San Francisco Peninsula is dominated by San Francisco and its spectacular Bay. Golden Gate Park, in a class with any of the world's finest urban parks, offers a virtual cornucopia of activities, including art and natural history museums, the Aquarium, arboretums, and numerous lakes and athletic fields. Cycling through the city along its busy streets, while sometimes hectic with the flow of car traffic, offers spectacular views and many cultural and historic points of interest.

Woodside and the MidPeninsula

Nestled in the foothills on the eastern slope of the Santa Cruz Mountains, the town of Woodside serves as a focal point for local cyclists and for those who have come from other places to cycle here. Easily one of the most popular cycling areas in all of northern California, Woodside offers numerous country roads with a wide variety of terrain, ranging from flat and gently rolling, to climbs sufficient to challenge even the most rugged riders. Recreational cyclists and top-level racing teams can commonly be seen sharing the roads on most weekends, as they cruise past the many local horse ranches and through the lush forests so typical of this area.

Along the Pacific Coast and on the Western Slope

In sharp contrast to the regions in the Santa Clara Valley, just over the mountains, the coast enjoys its own microclimate and remote country roads. On summer days, when the Valley is sweltering, it is not unusual for coastal communities to be shrouded in fog and blessed with temperatures 20 degrees lower. Farms, ranches and forests dominate the landscape, and car traffic along inland roads is almost non-existent. While there is considerable traffic on Highway 1, on the coast, an adequate shoulder is available for cycling safety.

Palo Alto and the Lower Peninsula

Palo Alto, the home of Stanford University and the cradle of the high-technology revolution which spawned "Silicon Valley," is a cycling mecca for the urban and suburban dwellers who live in the vicinity. It was, in fact, one of the first cities to recognize the value of bicycle transportation and to establish an extensive network of bike lanes along local streets. Through pleasant residential neighborhoods and the architecturally fascinating Stanford campus, and along the many peaceful country roads in the foothills, cyclists can experience relative remoteness, even when very near to the population centers of the Valley.

THE SAN FRANCISCO PENINSULA

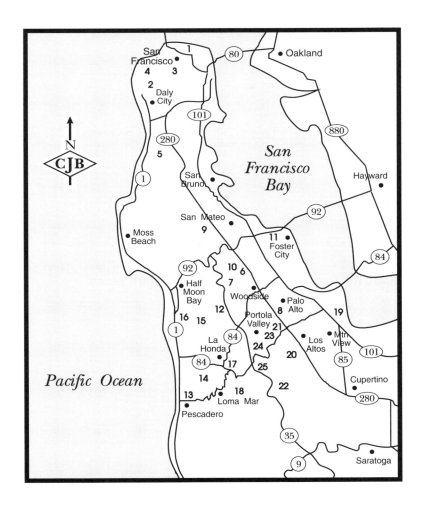

HOW TO USE THIS BOOK

Ride Parameters

At the beginning of each ride description is a short list of ride parameters. These are intended to give you a quick summary of that particular ride and to permit you to sort through the rides to find the one that best suits your needs.

Ride Rating — Reflects the overall difficulty of the ride, a simple judgment and classification into one of three possible categories: *Easy, Moderate,* or *Difficult.* This usually depends upon the distance and the total elevation gain of the ride, but can also be affected by the steepness of the hills.

Total Distance — Indicates the length of the ride, excluding any optional side trips which may be described in the ride.

Riding Time — Gives an indication of how much time to budget for the ride. Keep in mind, however, that this does not include extended stops for sightseeing, eating, and resting. The riding time usually assumes an average pace of about 8-10 miles per hour.

Total Elevation Gain — Combines the elevation gains of all the climbing required. For example, climbing two hills, each with 500 feet of elevation gain, would result in 1000 feet of total elevation gain.

Calories Burned — Estimates the total amount of energy burned. This is based upon an average calorie burn rate of about 300 calories per hour on a flat road at about 14 miles per hour and about 800 calories per hour on a hill climb, with about 8% grade and a speed of about 4 miles per hour. Some variations will occur for individual differences or for external factors.

Type of Bike — Suggests the use of a road or mountain bike. Although a ride may have a stretch of dirt road, it may still be suitable for a road bike, providing it is smooth and safe. Elaboration on this issue is usually found in the ride description.

Terrain

The general terrain and road conditions are briefly described to permit you to quickly determine if the ride is right for you. The best time of year for taking the ride is also provided to enhance your riding enjoyment.

Ride Description

This section gives a general description of the ride, along with any interesting background or historical information for the area. Points of interest along the way are highlighted as well. The general route to be followed is explained, although the details are saved for the *Ride*

Details and Mile Markers section. Extra side trips or variations of the basic ride are also included.

Starting Point

The exact place to start the ride is described, along with detailed directions for getting there. In general, rides are started at locations where free parking is readily available and where refreshments can be purchased either before or after your ride. Typically, the starting points are also easily recognizable places for groups of people meeting for a ride together.

Elevation Profiles

Elevation profiles for each ride provide a detailed view of the required hill climbs. These not only preview the ride for you, but can serve as a useful reference on your ride, since they can help you to anticipate the terrain and prepare you for the hills you will encounter.

Maps

Each ride has a map associated with it indicating the route. Rides with more than one option are indicated with direction arrows for each. In general, however, the map is not necessary for following the route, since detailed directions are included in the *Ride Details and Mile Markers* section. For clarity, the starting point of each ride is indicated on the map by an asterisk enclosed by a circle.

Ride Details and Mile Markers

Directions for the route are described, along with the elapsed distance for each item. You won't need a cycle computer since the markers come at frequent intervals, and you will quickly learn to estimate distances accurately enough. The markers indicate the required turns to take in order to follow the route and point out special sights and features of the ride that you might otherwise miss.

Ride Variations

Some ride routes offer several variations which have been given an A, B, or C suffix to distinguish them, such as 13A or 13B. In most cases, these variations are offered to give the rider different levels of difficulty from which to choose. Separate *Ride Details and Mile Markers* for each variation ensures that there is no confusion about the ride directions and essentially results in each variation being treated as a separate ride.

San Francisco
and the Upper Peninsula

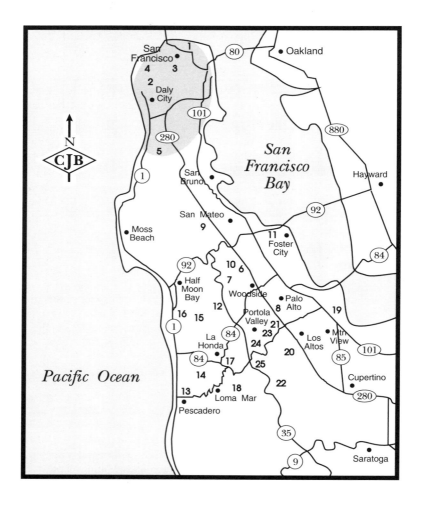

1 San Francisco
San Francisco to Tiburon with Ferry Return

Region: *San Francisco*
Total Distance: *18 miles*
Total Elevation Gain: *400 feet*
Type of Bike: *Road Bike*

Ride Rating: *Moderate*
Riding Time: *2-3 hours*
Calories Burned: *500*

Terrain

The ride is basically flat except for a climb necessary to cross the Golden Gate Bridge. Although car traffic will be encountered on the roads, much of the ride is on paved multi-use trails. Keep in mind, however, that these trails are shared by joggers, pedestrians and cyclists, so caution is required at all times.

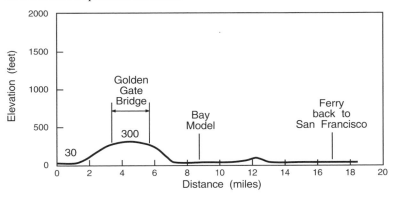

Ride Description

Stunning views of San Francisco and an exhilarating cruise on the Red & White Fleet Ferry highlight this delightful ride. Starting from the Marina Green, the route takes you along the waterfront and into the Presidio, from where you will climb a hill to cross the Golden Gate Bridge. Once across the bridge, you will descend into the charming town of Sausalito, where shops and restaurants abound. You will continue through Sausalito and onto a paved multi-use pathway which will take you along the water and through the mudflats. After a short length on roads, you will again get on a paved path for the final stretch into Tiburon.

In Tiburon, you will find restaurants, shops, and art galleries for diversion while you await the arrival of the ferry for your return to the city. Although the ferry runs on a frequent schedule, you may want to call in advance for departure times. The phone number for the Red & White Fleet is (415) 546-2896. The ferry crosses San Francisco Bay and terminates at Fishermen's Wharf, from where you will return to the Marina Green along surface roads.

Starting Point

Start the ride at the Marina Green Park, located between Fort Mason and the San Francisco Yacht Harbor. To get there, take the Civic Center exit off Highway 101 and follow Van Ness Avenue toward Fishermen's Wharf and Aquatic Park. Turn left on Bay Street, right on Laguna Street, and then left on Marina Boulevard. The Marina Green is on the right, along the Bay, where public parking and restrooms are available.

At the Harbor in Tiburon

Ride Details and Mile Markers

0.0 Start ride by heading WEST along Marina Boulevard.

0.4 Yacht Harbor on the right side.

0.7 Go STRAIGHT ahead off the road to enter Crissy Field on Mason Street.

1.1 Turn LEFT onto Halleck and go into the Presidio.

1.3 Turn RIGHT onto Lincoln Blvd.

1.4 Bear RIGHT to stay on Lincoln Blvd. View of Golden Gate Bridge directly ahead.

2.9 Pass under the approach to the Golden Gate Bridge.

3.1 Turn RIGHT on Merchant Road (Ralston Avenue is on the left).

3.3 Turn LEFT just before the highway and go through the underpass under the bridge toll booth. Continue THROUGH the parking lot and around to the right to get on the bridge. There are signs indicating that bicycles must use the west side of the bridge on weekends and may use the east side on weekdays.

5.3 Continue THROUGH the parking lot on the north end of the bridge and turn RIGHT onto Alexander Avenue, heading down the hill toward Sausalito.

6.7 Turn RIGHT onto Second Street toward Sausalito.

6.9 Turn RIGHT onto Richardson Street and then LEFT onto Bridgeway Road along the edge of the water.

7.4 Downtown Sausalito.

7.5 Sausalito Yacht Harbor on the right.

7.8 Bike path begins on the right side of the roadway.

8.1 Bike path diverges from the road side — easy to miss.

8.4 Bay Model on the right. Open to the public free of charge Monday through Saturday, this scale model of the entire San Francisco Bay and Delta was built by the U.S. Army Corps of Engineers to help understand the changing nature of the Bay.

8.6 Turn LEFT to follow the road.

8.9 Turn LEFT on Harbor Drive and once again get on the bike path as it follows along Bridgeway Road.

10.2 Freeway underpass — Mount Tamalpais in view straight ahead.

11.8 Turn RIGHT onto East Blithedale Avenue at the end of the bike path.

12.5 Freeway overpass — begin Tiburon Boulevard.

13.4 Turn RIGHT onto Greenwood Cove Drive.

13.8 Richardson Bay Audubon Society on right side.

14.2 End of road — begin bike path.

16.4 End of bike path. Follow bike lane along Tiburon Boulevard.

16.8   Intersection with Main Street on the right. This is the heart of Tiburon. The ferry access is STRAIGHT across Main Street, on the right side. Tickets are purchased on board. Phone ahead for Red & White Fleet departure schedule at (415) 546-2896. The ferry will take you to Pier 43½ at Fishermen's Wharf, where you will depart and turn RIGHT onto Jefferson Street.

17.1   Turn LEFT onto Hyde Street and climb short hill.

17.2   Turn RIGHT onto Beach Street.

17.3   Turn LEFT onto Polk Street and then RIGHT onto North Point Street.

17.5   Turn LEFT onto Van Ness Avenue.

17.6   Turn RIGHT onto Bay Street. Fort Mason on the right side.

17.9   Turn RIGHT onto Laguna Street, continuing around Fort Mason.

18.1   Turn LEFT onto Marina Boulevard at the end of Laguna Street.

18.3   Marina Green on the right side — end of the ride.

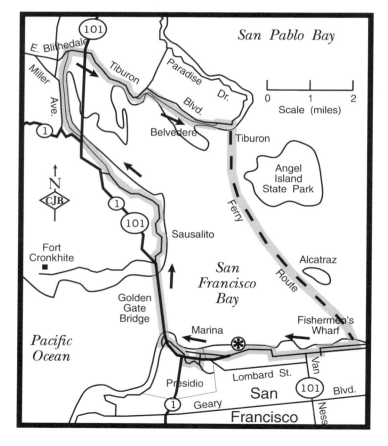

Ride No. 1

2 San Francisco
Golden Gate Park, Lake Merced and Twin Peaks

	Ride 2A	Ride 2B
Region:	San Francisco	
Ride Rating:	Easy	Moderate
Total Distance:	12 miles	18 miles
Riding Time:	2 hours	2 Hours
Total Elevation Gain:	200 feet	930 feet
Calories Burned:	300	600
Type of Bike:	Road Bike	Road Bike

Ride Description

Golden Gate Park, Lake Merced and Twin Peaks are highlights of this ride through the western part of San Francisco in the Sunset District. Both rides lead you through enchanting Golden Gate Park, and you will probably want to leave some extra time to explore the park after your ride. Lake Merced, located south of Golden Gate Park, in Harding Park, is near the superb San Francisco Zoo and historic Fort Funston. Spectacular panoramic views of the entire Bay Area are afforded from the summit of Twin Peaks in Ride 2B.

Starting Point

Start either ride at the west end of Golden Gate Park at the corner of John F. Kennedy Drive and the Great Highway, near the Murphy Windmill. Get there by way of 19th Avenue (Highway 1), turning off at the 25th Avenue exit and proceeding through the park to the west end at the ocean.

Ride 2A (Easy)

Ride 2A is an easy ride, following the Great Highway south from Golden Gate Park. After a loop around Lake Merced, the route returns to the park via tree-lined Sunset Boulevard, and then travels a short distance through the park to get back to the starting point.

Terrain

This ride is generally quite flat. Substantial car traffic may be encountered, however, so caution is advised at all times.

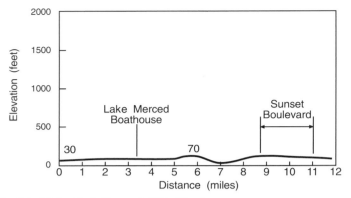

Ride 2A: Ride Details and Mile Markers

0.0 Proceed SOUTH on the Great Highway. Look for bike path on the left side (opposite the ocean).

2.5 Cross Sloat Boulevard. Bike path ends and you must ride in the road.

2.8 Climb small hill.

3.3 Turn LEFT onto Skyline Boulevard. Lake Merced — Harding Park will be on right side after the turn.

3.7 Turn RIGHT onto Lake Merced Boulevard.

4.2 Turn RIGHT where Sunset Boulevard intersects on the left to stay on Lake Merced Boulevard and continue around the lake.

6.2 Turn RIGHT onto John Muir Drive.

7.3 Bear RIGHT onto Skyline Boulevard once again.

7.8 Continue STRAIGHT at the intersection with the Great Highway on the left. At this point, you have completed the loop around Lake Merced.

8.5 Bear RIGHT to merge onto Sloat Boulevard.

8.7 Turn LEFT onto Sunset Boulevard.

10.9 Cross Lincoln Way to enter Golden Gate Park.

11.0 Turn LEFT onto Martin Luther King Drive.

11.8 Back at the starting point.

Ride 2B (Moderate)

Ride 2B begins by following the same route as Ride 2A, going south along the Great Highway and then looping around Lake Merced. After that, it heads east on Sloat Boulevard, north on Portola Drive, and then climbs Twin Peaks Boulevard toward the stunning views of the city available at the Twin Peaks viewing area (elevation 870 feet). The return to Golden Gate Park will bring you into the park at the east end and lead you through the entire park, back to where you started.

Terrain

This ride is predominantly on surface streets in San Francisco and, as a result, substantial car traffic will be encountered. Be certain to ride very carefully and to signal all your turns clearly. There is a significant hill climb leading to the Twin Peaks viewing area.

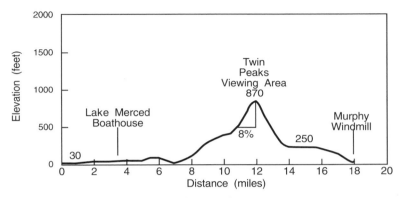

Ride 2B: Ride Details and Mile Markers

0.0 Proceed SOUTH on the Great Highway. Look for bike path on the left side (opposite the ocean).

2.5 Cross Sloat Boulevard. Bike path ends and you must ride in the road.

2.8 Climb small hill.

3.3 Turn LEFT onto Skyline Boulevard. Lake Merced — Harding Park will be on right side after the turn.

3.7 Turn RIGHT onto Lake Merced Boulevard.

4.2 Turn RIGHT where Sunset Boulevard intersects on the left to stay on Lake Merced Boulevard and continue around the lake.

6.2 Turn RIGHT onto John Muir Drive.

7.3 Bear RIGHT onto Skyline Boulevard once again.

7.8 Continue STRAIGHT at the intersection with the Great Highway on the left. At this point, you have completed the loop around Lake Merced.

8.5 Bear RIGHT to merge onto Sloat Boulevard.

9.7 Cross 19th Avenue.

9.9 Turn LEFT onto Portola Drive. Do not turn sharply left onto West Portal Avenue.

11.4 Turn LEFT onto Twin Peaks Boulevard, following signs for 49 Mile Scenic Route. Steep climb immediately.

12.6 Turn RIGHT at the summit to get to the viewing area. Summit — 870 feet.

12.8   Turn RIGHT to get back on Twin Peaks Boulevard and to go out at the opposite end from which you entered.

13.6   Turn RIGHT at Clarendon Avenue intersection to stay on Twin Peaks Boulevard.

13.8   Turn LEFT onto Carmel Street, being careful not to miss the turn.

14.0   Turn RIGHT onto Schrader Street and then LEFT onto 17th Street.

14.2   Turn RIGHT onto Stanyan Street.

14.9   Turn LEFT onto John F. Kennedy Drive through Golden Gate Park. This is the main road into the park and can be identified by the tree-lined boulevard, Fell Street, which goes to the right.

15.0   Bear RIGHT at the road split to stay on JFK Drive.

15.6   Conservatory of Flowers on the right side.

15.9   Rose Garden on the right side.

16.3   Cross under 19th Avenue.

18.0   Turn RIGHT at stop sign at end of road to stay on JFK Blvd.

18.3   Murphy Windmill on the right side, just before the Great Highway.

18.4   Back at the starting point.

Conservatory of Flowers in Golden Gate Park

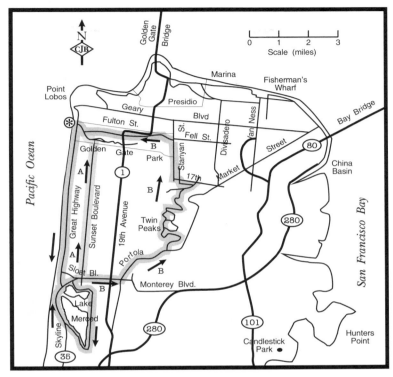

Ride No. 2

3 San Francisco

Waterfront, Presidio and Golden Gate Park

Region: *San Francisco*	**Ride Rating:** *Moderate*
Total Distance: *19 miles*	**Riding Time:** *2 hours*
Total Elevation Gain: *800 feet*	**Calories Burned:** *600*
Type of Bike: *Road Bike*	

Terrain

Busy surface streets of San Francisco make this ride one which requires special caution. Be sure to clearly signal all turns and other actions to passing cars. Some hills are encountered, the most significant ones being the climb through the Presidio and past the California Palace of the Legion of Honor, toward the end of the ride.

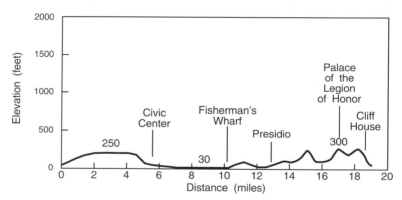

Ride Description

This ride explores several of the most popular tourist attractions in San Francisco. The route begins with a leisurely cruise through Golden Gate Park. Following city streets, you will then ride by the Civic Center and through town to the waterfront at the deep-water piers. Continuing along the water's edge, you will pass the Pier 39 tourist center, Fishermen's Wharf, and Fort Mason, on the way to the Marina district, where breathtaking views of the Golden Gate Bridge await you. Once past the marina, you will enter the Presidio and climb the hill, crossing directly under the approach to the Golden Gate Bridge. You will then pass through Lincoln Park and the California Palace of the Legion of Honor before you reach the coast. The final stretch takes you past the ruins of the Sutro Baths, the Cliff House, and then the final descent to the Great Highway and your starting point.

Starting Point

Start the ride at the west end of Golden Gate Park at the corner of John F. Kennedy Drive and the Great Highway, near the Murphy Windmill. Get there by way of 19th Avenue (Highway 1), turning off at the 25th Avenue exit and proceeding through the park to the west end at the Pacific Ocean.

Ride Details and Mile Markers

0.0   Proceed EAST onto JFK Drive into Golden Gate Park at the windmill. The street is unmarked.

0.4   Turn LEFT at the stop sign to stay on JFK Drive (not marked).

0.9   Buffalo pen on the left side.

2.0   Cross under 19th Avenue.

2.5   Rose Garden on the left side.

3.1   Conservatory of Flowers on the left side.

3.5   Continue STRAIGHT on Fell Street, heading east from Golden Gate Park.

4.2   Turn LEFT onto Baker Street.

4.4   Turn RIGHT onto Grove Street.

4.6   Turn LEFT onto Scott Street.

4.7   Turn RIGHT onto Fulton Street.

5.5   Turn LEFT onto Franklin Street.

5.6   Turn RIGHT onto McAllister Street. Civic Center on the right side.

5.9   Turn RIGHT onto Hyde Street.

6.1   Cross Market Street — becomes Eighth Street.

6.2   Turn LEFT onto Mission Street.

7.8   Turn RIGHT onto Steuart Street.

8.0   Turn LEFT onto Folsom Street.

8.1   Turn LEFT onto The Embarcadero.

9.0   Telegraph Hill and Coit Tower off to the left side.

9.7   Pier 39 shopping and tourist area on the right side.

10.0   Fisherman's Wharf on the right side. Begin Jefferson Street.

10.3   Turn LEFT onto Hyde Street and climb short hill.

10.4   Turn RIGHT onto Beach Street.

10.5   Turn LEFT onto Polk Street and then RIGHT onto North Point Street.

10.7   Turn LEFT onto Van Ness Avenue.

11.0   Turn RIGHT onto Bay Street. Fort Mason on the right side.

11.1   Turn RIGHT onto Laguna Street, continuing around Fort Mason.

11.3   Turn LEFT onto Marina Boulevard at the end of Laguna Street.

11.5   Marina Green on the right side.

11.9 Yacht harbor on the right side.

12.2 Go STRAIGHT ahead off the road to enter Crissy Field on Mason Street.

12.6 Turn LEFT onto Halleck and go into the Presidio.

12.8 Turn RIGHT onto Lincoln Blvd.

12.9 Bear RIGHT to stay on Lincoln Blvd. View of Golden Gate Bridge directly ahead.

14.4 Pass under the approach to the Golden Gate Bridge and begin climb.

15.0 Top of hill — 300 feet. Great views off to the right.

16.0 Begin El Camino Del Mar.

16.2 Bear LEFT to stay on El Camino Del Mar.

16.9 Bear LEFT to go past the California Palace of the Legion of Honor. Summit — 300 feet.

17.4 Turn RIGHT onto Clement Street, at the bottom of the hill.

17.7 Top of hill — 300 feet.

17.8 Begin Seal Rock Drive.

18.2 Turn LEFT onto El Camino Del Mar and then turn RIGHT onto Point Lobos Avenue.

18.5 Cliff House on the right. Begin descent to the Great Highway.

19.1 Back at the starting point.

View of the Golden Gate Bridge from Lincoln Park

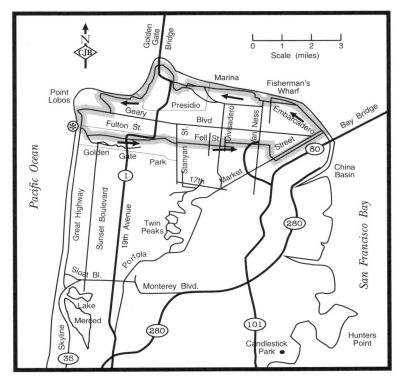

Ride No. 3

4

San Francisco
Tour of Golden Gate Park

Region: *San Francisco*
Total Distance: *12 miles*
Total Elevation Gain: *200 feet*
Type of Bike: *Road Bike*

Ride Rating: *Easy*
Riding Time: *1-2 hours*
Calories Burned: *300*

Terrain

The roads around Golden Gate Park are flat and wide, although there is an ever-so-slight uphill as one travels into the park from the westernmost end. Weekends usually find the park very crowded with tourists and locals enjoying the many diversions within it. Sundays are especially delightful for cycling, since the roads within the park are closed to car traffic.

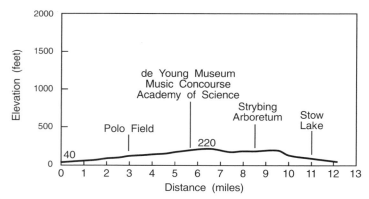

Ride Description

Golden Gate Park serves as a superb example of what an urban park can be. Reclaimed from barren land dominated by scrub oak and sand dunes, the park was constructed beginning in 1870. The addition of topsoil and the planting of a wide variety of plants and trees began the conversion of the land into what today serves as the centerpiece of the San Francisco Recreation and Park Department system.

Encompassing an area about three miles long and ½-mile wide, it contains the M.H. de Young Memorial Museum, Asian Art Museum, and California Academy of Sciences (with the Steinhart Aquarium, Morrrison Planetarium, and the Hall of Man natural history museum). In addition, the Japanese Tea Garden, Conservatory of Flowers, Strybing Arboretum and Botanical Gardens combine to add a natural flavor to the man-made efforts displayed in the museums. Scattered throughout the park are numerous lakes, meadows, and paths for relaxing and reflecting.

Spreckels Lake is the home of the San Francisco Model Yacht Club and it is not unusual to find the lake occupied by miniature versions of classic racing boats. Paddle boats and rowboats can be rented at Stow Lake and free outdoor concerts are often performed by the Golden Gate Park Band on Sunday afternoons in the Music Concourse.

This ride takes you on a casual tour around the park, passing by nearly all of the major attractions. Be sure to bring your bike lock and be prepared to spend a lot of time discovering the many pleasures of this wonderful park.

Starting Point

Start the ride at the west end of Golden Gate Park at the corner of John F. Kennedy Drive and the Great Highway, near the Murphy Windmill. Get there by way of 19th Avenue (Highway 1), turning off at the 25th Avenue exit and proceeding through the park to the west end at the Pacific Ocean.

M.H. deYoung Museum in Golden Gate Park

Ride Details and Mile Markers

0.0   Proceed EAST on John F. Kennedy Drive, away from the ocean and into the park.

0.3   Continue STRAIGHT at the stop sign.

0.4   Continue STRAIGHT to merge with Martin Luther King Drive, coming in on the right.

0.7   Continue STRAIGHT at the stop sign — South Lake on the left just after this intersection.

0.9   Bear RIGHT at the split in the road to stay on MLK Drive.

0.9   Continue STRAIGHT at the stop sign (Sunset Boulevard is to the right).

2.1   Turn LEFT onto Middle Drive West just before the 19th Avenue intersection.

2.2   Bear LEFT to stay on Middle Drive West.

3.0   Continue STRAIGHT at the stop sign to stay on Middle Drive West — Polo Field on the right.

3.3   Turn RIGHT onto MLK Drive.

3.5   Turn RIGHT at stop sign onto Chain of Lakes Drive — follow 49 Mile Scenic Route sign. Bercut Equitation Field on the left shortly after the turn.

3.7   Turn RIGHT onto John F. Kennedy Drive — follow 49 Mile Scenic Route sign.

3.8   Buffalo Pen on the left.

4.1   Riding Academy on the right.

5.0   19th Avenue underpass.

5.5   Rose Garden on the left.

5.7   Turn RIGHT on Hagiwara Tea Garden Drive toward M.H. de Young Museum and Japanese Tea Garden.

5.8   M.H. de Young Museum on the right and Music Concourse on the left.

5.9   Hagiwara Japanese Tea Garden on the right.

6.0   Turn LEFT onto Martin Luther King Drive.

6.1   Turn LEFT toward the California Academy of Sciences and the Steinhart Aquarium.

6.4   Turn RIGHT to get back onto John F. Kennedy Drive.

6.7   Conservatory of Flowers on the left.

6.8   Turn RIGHT onto Bowling Green Drive.

6.9   Bear LEFT at intersection.

7.1   Lawn Bowling on the right.

7.2   Turn RIGHT onto Martin Luther King Drive.

7.4   Ball fields on the right.

7.5   Turn RIGHT to stay on MLK Drive.

7.6 Strybing Arboretum on the left.

7.8 Japanese Tea Garden again on the right.

8.2 Turn RIGHT toward Stow Lake.

8.7 Stow Lake Boathouse on the right.

8.8 Turn RIGHT just after boathouse to continue around Stow Lake.

9.3 Turn RIGHT to get back on MLK Drive.

9.6 Continue STRAIGHT across Nineteenth Avenue and then turn RIGHT immediately onto Middle Drive West.

9.8 Bear RIGHT at intersection to get on Transverse Drive.

10.0 Turn LEFT onto John F. Kennedy Drive.

10.1 Lloyd Lake on the right.

10.5 Lindley Meadow on the left.

10.8 Turn RIGHT at stop sign toward 30th Avenue and then turn LEFT immediately onto small paved trail, just before the park exit.

11.0 Spreckels Lake on the left.

11.2 Turn LEFT at stop sign and then turn RIGHT to get back on John F. Kennedy Drive — San Francisco Model Yacht Club Building on the right.

11.4 Buffalo Pen on the right.

11.6 Continue STRAIGHT at the stop sign.

12.0 Turn RIGHT at the stop sign at the end of JFK Drive.

12.3 Back at the start point.

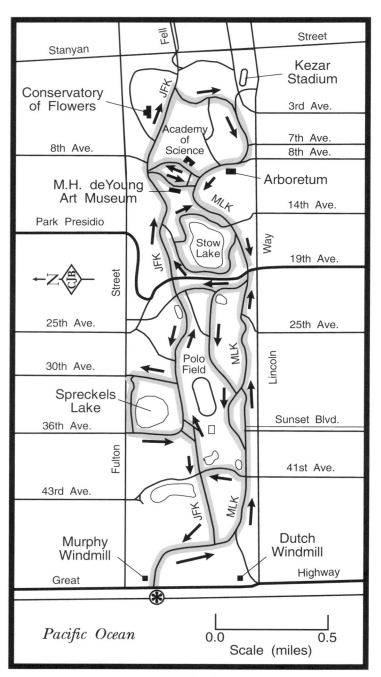

Ride No. 4

5 San Bruno
Sweeney Ridge

Region: *San Francisco*
Total Distance: *12 miles*
Total Elevation Gain: *1600 feet*
Type of Bike: *Mountain Bike*

Ride Rating: *Moderate*
Riding Time: *2 hours*
Calories Burned: *750*

Terrain

Road surfaces are paved, except for about 4 miles on dirt trails with some very steep downhill sections. Some traffic is encountered on a section of Highway 1 for about ½-mile. Two climbs are required, with one very steep section on Sneath Lane.

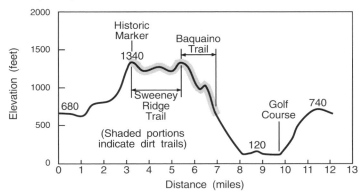

Ride Description

On November 4, 1769, the expedition of the Spanish explorer, Captain Gaspar de Portolá, in search of Monterey Bay, climbed from the coast to what is today Sweeney Ridge. From that vantage point, his party beheld the valley below and the present-day San Francisco Bay. Not realizing the importance of his discovery, Portolá and his group camped by a small lagoon, now covered over by San Andreas Lake, and attempted to get around the bay. Unsuccessful in that effort, he eventually found Monterey Bay in the following year. In 1773, subsequent Spanish expeditions charted the San Francisco Bay and established San Francisco.

Historic Sweeney Ridge, encompassing some 1047 acres, was incorporated into the Golden Gate National Recreation Area in 1984. At the top of Sweeney Ridge, you will find magnificent views to the east of the San Andreas Lake and the San Francisco Watershed, the Bay, and Mount Diablo, and to the west, of Pacifica and the ocean shoreline.

The route leads out of the Skyline College campus and through residential neighborhoods to Sneath Lane. At the end of Sneath Lane is the paved trail, also named Sneath Lane, leading to Sweeney Ridge. This trail is very steep in places and climbs about 600 feet to get to the ridge top. At the top, there is a small marker on the unpaved Sweeney Ridge Trail.

After proceeding out and back along Sweeney Ridge Trail, you will follow Baquaino Trail down the other side of the ridge to Pacifica. This is also unpaved and is very steep. Once in Pacifica, you will follow Highway 1 a short distance north and then return to the campus by climbing up Sharp Park Drive.

Starting Point

Skyline College, in San Bruno, is the starting point for the ride. There is plenty of parking on the campus, but during the week you must be careful to avoid parking areas requiring a permit. To get to the campus from the north, get off Highway 280 at Sneath Lane and follow Sneath Lane west to Skyline Boulevard. Turn right on Skyline Boulevard and proceed about ½-mile to the campus.

From the south, exit Highway 280 at the Skyline Boulevard and Pacifica off ramp. Follow Skyline Boulevard for about 2.5 miles to the campus. Start the mileage from the athletic field in the center of the campus.

Ride Details and Mile Markers

0.0 Proceed out of the campus on College Drive toward Skyline Boulevard.

0.5 Turn RIGHT onto Longview Drive.

0.6 Turn LEFT onto Moreland Drive.

0.8 Turn LEFT onto Riverside Drive.

0.9 Turn RIGHT onto Sneath Lane.

1.6 Continue STRAIGHT into Golden Gate National Recreation Area at the gate, heading toward Sweeney Ridge.

3.2 Turn LEFT at the top of the ridge onto unpaved Sweeney Ridge Trail.

3.3 A historical marker is located on the hilltop to the left of the trail with sweeping views of the bay to the east and the ocean to the west. Continue STRAIGHT on Sweeney Ridge Trail at the intersection with Baquaino Trail on the right.

4.4 Gate marking the end of Sweeney Ridge Trail. Turn around and return the way you came.

5.4 Turn LEFT onto Baquaino Trail. Be careful, since this is a very steep descent.

6.4 Go past gate and then turn LEFT toward Fassler Avenue.

6.9 Continue STRAIGHT at the gate onto paved Fassler Avenue.

8.2 Turn RIGHT onto Highway 1 (Coast Highway).

8.8 CROSS OVER Highway 1 to use the bike path on the west side of the roadway.

9.1 Follow bike route signs to avoid this section of the highway. You will follow parallel to the highway on Bradford Way, along the golf course.

9.7 Sharp Park Golf Course clubhouse on the left.

9.8 Turn RIGHT onto Sharp Park Road and cross over freeway.

11.1 Turn RIGHT onto College Drive toward Skyline College campus.

11.5 Enter campus and turn RIGHT to loop around.

12.1 End of the ride at the athletic field.

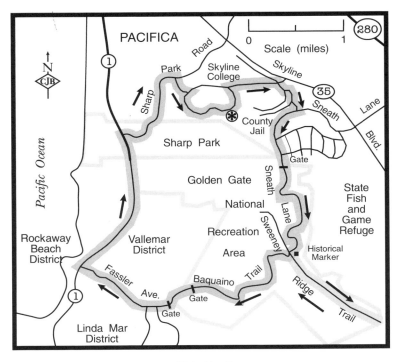

Ride No. 5

Woodside
and the Mid-Peninsula

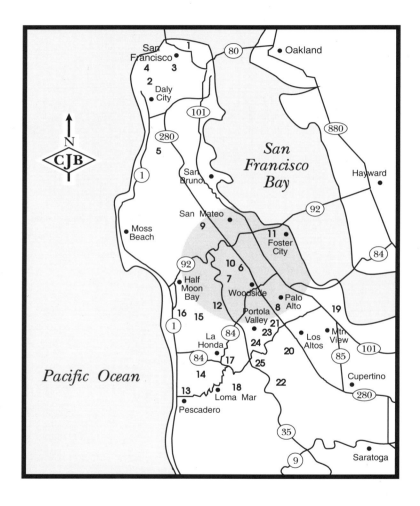

6 Portola Valley
Pulgas Water Temple

Region: *Mid-Peninsula*
Total Distance: *24 miles*
Total Elevation Gain: *800 feet*
Type of Bike: *Road Bike*

Ride Rating: *Moderate*
Riding Time: *3 hours*
Calories Burned: *600*

Terrain

Rolling hills with only a few relatively easy climbs best characterizes the terrain for this ride. Most roads have bike lanes for added safety.

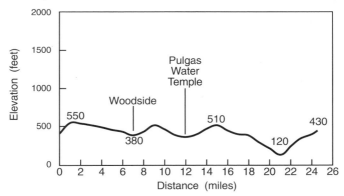

Ride Description

Far away from the Bay Area, within the boundaries of Yosemite National Park, lies the Tuolomne River watershed. Each year, in the springtime, when the Sierra snows melt and feed the many streams flowing into the Grand Canyon of the Tuolomne, the water accumulates behind the O'Shaughnessy Dam and forms the Hetch Hetchy Reservoir. Then, through a remarkable series of tunnels and powerhouses, the water is transported completely across the Central Valley and into Crystal Springs Reservoir, located just north of Woodside, to serve the needs of the Bay Area. As a monument to the accomplishment of this achievement, the Pulgas Water Temple reminds us of the precious nature of this resource.

This ride takes you from Portola Valley through the town of Woodside and along Cañada Road to the Pulgas Water Temple. Along the way, you will follow roads very popular with local cyclists, both for their natural beauty as well as for the general absence of extreme hills.

Starting Point

The ride starts in Portola Valley at the intersection of Alpine Road and Arastradero Road. To get there, take the Alpine Road exit from Interstate Highway 280 and proceed west on Alpine Road for about 1 mile to the intersection with Arastradero Road. A convenient meeting place is the Alpine Inn restaurant (formerly known as "Rossotti's"), a favorite of local cyclists and equestrians.

Ride Details and Mile Markers

0.0   Proceed WEST on Alpine Road, away from Highway 280.

1.1   Turn RIGHT onto Portola Road.

2.5   Portola Town Center on the left.

4.6   Turn LEFT to stay on Portola Road (at Sand Hill Road intersection).

4.8   Turn RIGHT onto Mountain Home Road.

6.8   Continue STRAIGHT at the intersection with Woodside Road (Highway 84) at the town of Woodside to begin Cañada Road.

8.1   Freeway underpass.

9.7   Another freeway underpass.

10.3 Edgewood Road intersection on the right.

11.9 Turn LEFT into Pulgas Water Temple parking lot. There are restrooms and pathways leading to the water temple. When you have completed your stay here, return on Cañada Road the way you came, heading back toward Woodside.

13.5 Edgewood Road intersection on the left.

14.1 Freeway underpass.

15.7 Another freeway underpass.

17.0 Turn LEFT onto Woodside Road (Highway 84).

17.2 Turn RIGHT onto Whiskey Hill Road.

18.6 Turn LEFT onto Sand Hill Road.

19.9 Freeway overpass.

21.0 Turn RIGHT onto Santa Cruz Avenue.

21.1 Junipero Serra Boulevard intersection on the left.

22.4 Freeway underpass.

24.3 Back at the start point.

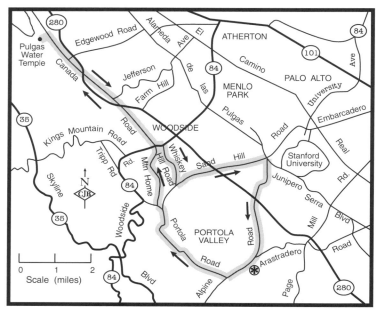

Ride No. 6

One of many historic buildings in Woodside

7 Woodside
Old La Honda Road

	Ride 7A	Ride 7B
Region:	*Mid-Peninsula*	
Ride Rating:	*Difficult*	*Difficult*
Total Distance:	*16 miles*	*21 miles*
Riding Time:	*2-3 hours*	*3-4 hours*
Total Elevation Gain:	*1400 feet*	*2200 feet*
Calories Burned:	*700*	*1000*
Type of Bike:	*Road Bike*	*Road Bike*

Ride Description

Both rides start in Woodside, a town originally noted for its proximity to logging operations in the mountains and for its use as a center of supplies and hotels for loggers. The route takes you by the historic Woodside Store, containing a museum with artifacts from old Woodside. Originally owned and operated by Robert O. Tripp, for whom the road in front is named, the store once served the many needs of the community, functioning as a post office, general store, hotel, stable, and gathering place for local residents.

Climbing up Old La Honda Road gives the opportunity to contemplate this former logging road, which today is one of the hidden gems of the backroads around the Bay Area. Free of the heavy traffic so typical of most roads in the area, Old La Honda Road winds steeply up to Skyline Boulevard through lush redwood forests.

Starting Point

To get to Woodside take the Woodside Road (State Highway 84) exit off of Interstate 280 and proceed west toward Woodside. Park anywhere in or near the town and start the ride at the intersection of Woodside Road and Mountain Home Road (Cañada Road on the opposite side of the intersection).

Ride 7A (Difficult)

After leaving town past the Woodside Store the route then climbs up Old La Honda Road (1700 feet elevation) and follows the mountain ridge along Skyline Boulevard. The return to Woodside is downhill on Woodside Road (Highway 84).

Terrain

There is a rather steep (8%) climb on Old La Honda Road, although the climb is free of the heavy traffic usually present on other roads in the area. Some traffic will be encountered on the descent back into Woodside on Woodside Road.

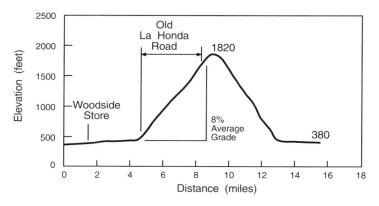

Ride 7A: Ride Details and Mile Markers

0.0 From Woodside, head WEST on Woodside Road (Highway 84), in the direction to take you through the town.

0.7 Turn RIGHT onto Kings Mountain Road.

1.4 Turn LEFT onto Tripp Road. Historic Woodside Store is at this intersection.

2.3 Turn RIGHT onto Woodside Road (Highway 84).

3.5 Turn LEFT onto Portola Road.

4.1 Bear RIGHT at the intersection with Mountain Home Road on the left.

4.3 Turn RIGHT at the intersection with Sand Hill Road on the left to stay on Portola Road.

4.8 Turn RIGHT onto Old La Honda Road.

8.3 Turn RIGHT onto Skyline Boulevard (Highway 35).

9.2 Crest — 1820 feet.

9.7 Turn RIGHT at the intersection with Woodside Road (Highway 84).

13.2 Portola Road intersection on right side.

14.3 Tripp Road intersection on left side.

14.8 Kings Mountain Road intersection on left side.

15.6 Back at Woodside.

Ride 7B   (Difficult)

Ride 7B also leaves town past the Woodside Store, Portola Road, and up Old La Honda Road. Instead of returning to Woodside down Woodside Road, however, you will continue on Skyline Boulevard to Kings Mountain Road, and return down that road.

Terrain

There is a rather steep (8%) climb on Old La Honda Road and a second climb on Skyline Boulevard. The descent on Kings Mountain Road is winding, but will usually present very little car traffic.

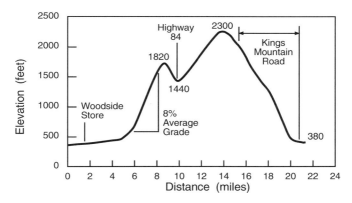

Ride 7B: Ride Details and Mile Markers

0.0   From Woodside, head WEST on Woodside Road (Highway 84), in the direction to take you through the town.

0.7   Turn RIGHT onto Kings Mountain Road.

1.4   Turn LEFT onto Tripp Road. Historic Woodside Store is at this intersection.

2.3   Turn RIGHT onto Woodside Road (Highway 84).

3.5   Turn LEFT onto Portola Road.

4.1   Bear RIGHT at the intersection with Mountain Home Road on the left.

4.3   Turn RIGHT at the intersection with Sand Hill Road on the left to stay on Portola Road.

4.8   Turn RIGHT onto Old La Honda Road.

8.3   Turn RIGHT onto Skyline Boulevard (Highway 35).

9.2   Crest — 1820 feet.

9.7   Continue STRAIGHT at the intersection with Woodside Road (Highway 84).

14.1   Crest — 2300 feet.

15.3 Turn RIGHT onto Kings Mountain Road and begin winding descent.
18.3 Huddart Park on the left.
19.7 Woodside Store on the right.
20.4 Turn LEFT onto Woodside Road.
21.1 Back at Woodside.

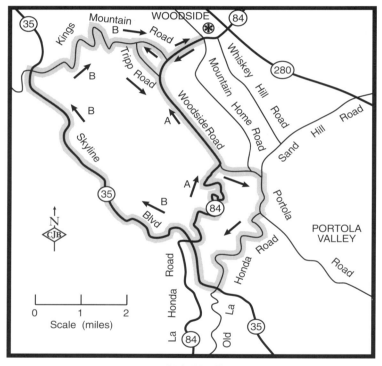

Ride No. 7

8 Los Altos
Kings Mountain Road

Region: *Mid-Peninsula*
Total Distance: *43 miles*
Total Elevation Gain: *3400 feet*
Type of Bike: *Road Bike*

Ride Rating: *Difficult*
Riding Time: *4-5 hours*
Calories Burned: *1700*

Terrain

The roads are generally lightly traveled. Two big climbs are encountered: the first is a 1600-foot ascent up Kings Mountain Road in Woodside, and the second is a 700-foot climb along Skyline Boulevard. Outstanding views of the Santa Clara Valley and the variety of roadside scenes reward you for the effort of this truly exceptional ride.

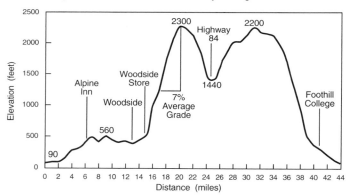

Ride Description

The town of Los Altos serves as the starting point for the ride. Along Main Street in Los Altos are numerous restaurants and shops beckoning you to browse. The ride begins with a leisurely cruise through part of Los Altos Hills (whose name is an interesting redundancy) and then gains elevation slightly along Arastradero Road through Palo Alto. Climbing some more on Alpine Road and following a level section on Portola Road takes you through Woodside, a town whose charm is a throwback to its early history as a commercial logging center.

Just out of town, the major hill climb of the ride begins up Kings Mountain Road, a five mile section which gains about 1600 feet in elevation. At the top of Kings Mountain Road, the climb is not yet complete until another 300 feet of elevation gain on Skyline Boulevard has been achieved. An exhilarating descent along Skyline Boulevard to the intersection with Woodside Road is followed by another climb, this one with a gain of about 700 feet in elevation. The final descent along Page Mill Road and Moody Road leads you past horse ranches and through the campus of Foothill College and finally back to Los Altos.

Starting Point

Start the ride in downtown Los Altos. There is ample parking in the parking lot in the rear of the stores on Main Street. To get there, take Interstate Highway 280 to the El Monte Road exit and head east on El Monte toward Los Altos. Turn left on Foothill Expressway and follow it for about 1 mile to Main Street. Turn right on Main Street and park anywhere around town. Begin the ride at the corner of Main Street and 3rd Street.

Ride Details and Mile Markers

0.0 Proceed on Main Street toward Foothill Expressway.

0.2 Continue STRAIGHT across Foothill Expressway.

0.3 Turn RIGHT onto Old Los Altos Road.

0.4 Turn RIGHT onto Fremont Road.

1.5 Bear RIGHT to stay on Fremont Road (at Concepcion Road intersection).

2.4 Turn LEFT onto Arastradero Road.

3.3 Cross under Highway 280 and begin short climb.

3.9 Turn LEFT onto Page Mill Road.

4.2 Turn RIGHT to get back on Arastradero Road.

4.7 Arastradero Preserve on right side.

6.2 Turn LEFT onto Alpine Road.

7.3 Turn RIGHT onto Portola Road.

10.8 Turn LEFT to stay on Portola Road (at Sand Hill Road intersection).

11.0 Turn RIGHT onto Mountain Home Road.

13.0 Turn LEFT onto Highway 84 (Woodside Road).

13.8 Turn RIGHT onto Kings Mountain Road.

14.5 Historic Woodside Store and museum on the left side.

14.6 Begin climb.

15.9 Huddart Park on the right side.

18.9 Turn LEFT onto Skyline Blvd.

20.1 Crest of hill.

24.5 Continue STRAIGHT at Highway 84 (La Honda Road) intersection.

26.7 Views off both left and right sides.

31.9 Turn LEFT onto Page Mill Road.

32.5 Monte Bello Open Space Preserve on the right side.

37.9 Turn RIGHT onto Moody Road.

40.7 Continue STRAIGHT into Foothill College campus at intersection with Elena Road on the left.

40.9 Turn RIGHT at stop sign.

41.0 Turn RIGHT in middle of campus to get to exit.

41.1 Turn LEFT onto El Monte Road.

41.4 Cross under Highway 280.

42.2 Turn LEFT on Foothill Expressway.

42.5 Turn RIGHT on San Antonio Road.

42.8 Turn LEFT onto Whitney Street and then RIGHT onto Third Street.

42.9 Back at the starting point.

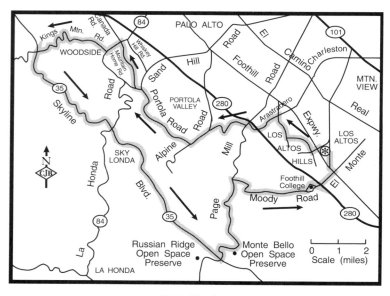

Ride No. 8

9

San Mateo
Sawyer Camp Trail

Region: *Mid-Peninsula*
Total Distance: *12 miles*
Total Elevation Gain: *250 feet*
Type of Bike: *Road Bike*

Ride Rating: *Easy*
Riding Time: *1-2 hours*
Calories Burned: *300*

Terrain

This is a generally flat ride along a paved multi-use trail, except for a small climb near the end of the trail. The trail is 6 miles long and the return is along the same route. Because of the heavy use of this very popular trail (pedestrians, runners, and cyclists), especially on weekends, it is imperative that great caution is exercised at all times.

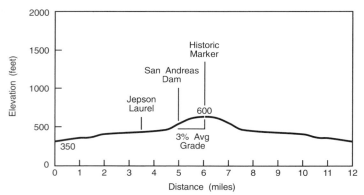

Ride Description

Around the year 1400, considerably before Columbus set sail for America, a particular tree was beginning its life in what is now Northern California. Populated by Shalshone Indians, the area around the tree was in a truly pristine state, untouched by the progress and ravages of modern man.

Some time later, in 1769, when the famous Spanish explorer, Don Gaspar de Portolà, became the first white man to set eyes on San Francisco Bay from Sweeney Ridge, that same California Laurel tree (also known as a Bay Tree) was then over 400 years old and stood witness to the event, although albeit at some distance. Today that tree, known as the Jepson Laurel, still stands, only now it is passed weekly by thousands of people as they relax and unwind from the tensions of modern life by traversing the Sawyer Camp Trail.

If trees could talk, this one could also tell the story of a man named Leander Sawyer who, in 1853, some 84 years after Portolà, bought the land around the area and established a trail leading to his home. Later, the trail was used for stagecoaches and ultimately became part of the main route between San Francisco and Half Moon Bay. After the flooding of Crystal Springs Reservoir in 1888 to serve the water needs of San Francisco, the road was used very little until 1978, when it was made into a recreation trail.

The Jepson Laurel, named in honor of Willis Linn Jepson, a noted botanist in California, is one of the highlights of this casual ride. Be sure to stop at the picnic site along the Sawyer Camp Trail to soak up the atmosphere around this famous tree.

Starting Point

The Sawyer Camp Trail starts at the Lower Crystal Springs Reservoir in San Mateo, at the intersection of Crystal Springs Road and Skyline Boulevard. To get there, take the Highway 92 exit off Interstate Highway 280 and head west toward Half Moon Bay. After about ½-mile, turn right on Skyline Boulevard (Highway 35). Stay on Skyline Boulevard about 1.5 miles to the intersection with Crystal Springs Road, on the right. The entrance to Sawyer Camp Trail is at this intersection.

Sawyer Camp Trail

Ride Details and Mile Markers

- 0.0   Proceed on the Sawyer Camp Trail by entering past the gate.
- 3.5   Picnic Area on the left side. Jepson Laurel, the oldest and largest known laurel tree in California, is located here.
- 4.8   Begin to climb.
- 5.1   Cross over San Andreas Dam.
- 5.9   Information board on the left side.
- 6.0   Gate at the north end of the trail. Historic marker is located just past the gate. Return on the trail the way you came.
- 6.9   Cross back over dam.
- 8.5   Picnic area on the right.
- 12.0   Back at the start point.

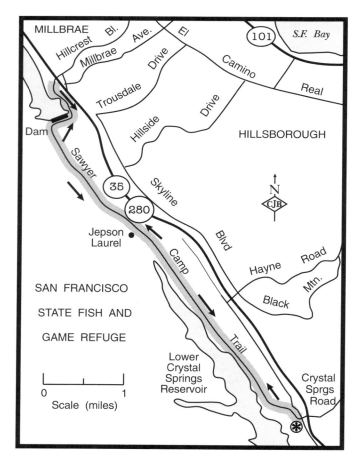

Ride No. 9

10 Woodside
Cañada Road — Skyline Blvd — Kings Mountain Loop

Region: *Mid-Peninsula*
Total Distance: *23 miles*
Total Elevation Gain: *2000 feet*
Type of Bike: *Road Bike*

Ride Rating: *Difficult*
Riding Time: *3 hours*
Calories Burned: *1000*

Terrain

There is some car traffic to contend with on this ride which includes a 3-mile stretch on busy Highway 92 and about 8 miles on Skyline Boulevard. The majority of the climb is on Skyline Boulevard, but the grade is modest (about 5%) and there is an adequate shoulder. Descending on Kings Mountain Road will require some braking, since the grade is steep and there are plenty of curves. In the summer, Cañada Road is closed to car traffic on the first and third Sundays of each month.

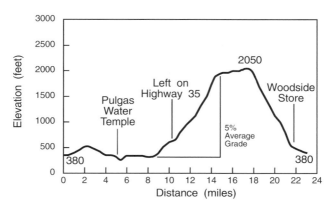

Ride Description

The San Andreas Fault is certainly one of the most famous in the world. It extends from the vicinity of Point Arena in Northern California all the way to Baja and passes directly through the Bay Area. San Andreas Lake and both Upper and Lower Crystal Springs Reservoirs lie directly along the fault line. The fault is actually a split between two major sections of the Earth's crust and undergoes steady movement, with the Pacific Plate on the west moving north, relative to the American Plate on the east, about 1-2 inches per year.

Major earthquakes can occur when the plates fail to slip for extended periods of time and the resulting stresses build to the point where a major slip suddenly results. This was the case in 1906, when the Great San Francisco Earthquake, centered near Point Reyes, just north of San Francisco, occurred and the Pacific Plate lunged northward about 16 feet! The resulting shock waves traveled through the earth's core and were recorded all over the world.

The ride starts in the town of Woodside and follows Cañada Road generally along the fault line and past Lower Crystal Springs Reservoir. A short climb toward Half Moon Bay along busy Highway 92 is followed by a longer climb along the ridge of the Santa Cruz Mountains on Skyline Boulevard. Although it is not extremely steep, the climb on Skyline Boulevard is a long one and takes you to an elevation of about 2000 feet. The final descent back to Woodside is along windy Kings Mountain Road.

Starting Point

The ride starts in the town of Woodside. To get there, take the Woodside Road (State Highway 84) exit off of Interstate 280 and head toward Woodside. Park anywhere in or near the town and start the ride at the intersection of Highway 84 and Cañada Road.

Ride Details and Mile Markers

0.0   From Woodside, head NORTH on Cañada Road.

1.3   Cross under Highway 280.

2.9   Cross under Highway 280 again.

3.5   Edgewood Road intersection on the right.

4.7   Filoli Historic Center on the left.

5.1   Pulgas Water Temple on the left.

7.5   Turn LEFT onto Highway 92.

8.2   Intersection with Highway 35 on the right.

8.4   Begin climb.

10.2   Turn LEFT onto Highway 35 (Skyline Blvd).

14.6   Kings Mountain Store on the right.

14.7   Purisima Creek Redwoods Open Space Preserve on the right.

16.0   Mountain House Restaurant on the right.

17.2   Turn LEFT onto Kings Mountain Road and begin winding descent.

20.2   Huddart Park on the left.

21.6   Historic Woodside Store and museum on the right.

22.3   Turn LEFT onto Highway 84 (Woodside Road).

23.1   Back at Woodside.

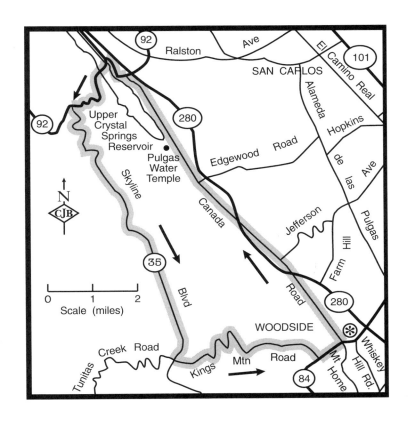

Ride No. 10

11 San Mateo
Foster City and San Mateo Bikeways

	Ride 11A	Ride 11B
Region:	*Mid-Peninsula*	
Ride Rating:	*Easy*	*Easy*
Total Distance:	*9 miles*	*14 miles*
Riding Time:	*1-2 hours*	*1-2 hours*
Total Elevation Gain:	*20 feet*	*40 feet*
Calories Burned:	*250*	*400*
Type of Bike:	*Road Bike*	*Road Bike*

Ride Description

Ride 11A is a loop around Foster City, a planned community built in 1959 on landfill surrounding what was then Brewer Island. Formerly salt ponds owned by noted salt companies, Schilling and Leslie, the city now houses almost 30,000 residents. The Foster City Bikeway/Pedway is a multi-use route, serving the enjoyment of pedestrians, joggers and cyclists.

Ride 11B is an out-and-back ride along the San Mateo Pedway/Bikeway. A highlight is Coyote Point, about 3.5 miles into the ride. At Coyote Point are a picturesque yacht harbor and pier, as well as the Coyote Point Museum. Open to the public for a nominal fee, the museum offers an informative introduction to the ecology, natural history, and environmental concerns of the bay.

Starting Point

Start each ride in San Mateo, near the Fashion Island Shopping Center, at the intersection of Fashion Island Boulevard and Mariners Island Boulevard. To get there, take Highway 101 (Bayshore Freeway) to the Hillsdale Boulevard exit in Foster City. Follow Hillsdale Boulevard east to Edgewater Boulevard. Turn left on Edgewater Boulevard (which becomes Mariners Island Boulevard) to the intersection with Fashion Island Boulevard. Park anywhere nearby and begin mileage at the corner.

Ride 11A (Easy)

This ride loops around Foster City along a lagoon and then along the Belmont Slough (pronounced "slew"), before reaching the levee along San Franicsco Bay. At the Highway 92 bridge, there is a fishing pier extending out into the Bay accessible by bicycle. The final return to the starting point also follows surface streets with a bike lane for safety.

Terrain

This is an easy ride along the totally flat Foster City Pedway/Bikeway, but prevailing northerly headwinds can make it seem like an uphill climb, at least when heading into the wind. The pathway is used by pedestrians as well as cyclists, so it is important to be careful and courteous.

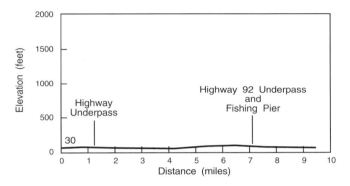

Ride 11A: Ride Details and Mile Markers

0.0   From the intersection of Fashion Island Boulevard and Mariners Island Boulevard, head WEST on Fashion Island Boulevard.

0.2   Turn LEFT to get on the Foster City Pedway/Bikeway, just before the bridge.

0.3   Highway 92 underpass.

1.2   Highway 92 underpass.

2.5   Continue STRAIGHT at bikeway intersection off to the right.

4.9   Beach Park Boulevard on the left side of the bikeway.

7.1   Highway 92 underpass. Fishing pier on the right side.

8.5   Turn LEFT onto Mariners Island Boulevard. Cross road by walking your bike in the pedestrian crosswalk.

9.4   Back at the start point.

Ride 11B (Easy)

This ride follows surface streets for only a short distance before beginning the Foster City Pedway/Bikeway. It is an out-and-back tour along the shoreline.

Terrain

This is a flat ride with frequently windy conditions prevailing. The route follows a multi-use pathway, available for use by pedestrians, as well as cyclists, so extra care must be taken to avoid collisions. Some surface street riding is required in both directions on this out-and-back route.

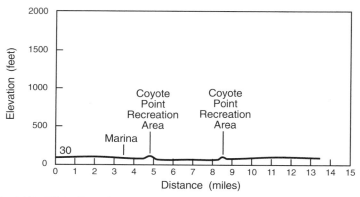

Ride 11B: Ride Details and Mile Markers

0.0 From the intersection of Fashion Island Boulevard and Mariners Island Boulevard, head NORTH on Mariners Island Boulevard.

0.9 Turn LEFT onto East Third Avenue and get on the San Mateo Pedway/Bikeway just off the road on the right side.

1.4 Cross over bridge.

1.7 Continue past gate and bear RIGHT to stay on bikeway, heading away from the road and toward the water.

2.5 Bear RIGHT, cross bridge, and then turn RIGHT to stay on the bikeway along the shoreline.

3.4 Turn RIGHT to continue on bikeway along water edge.

3.6 Bear LEFT at yacht harbor. Coyote Point Yacht Club building is on the left.

3.7 Cross road and stay on bikeway.

Coyote Point Yacht Harbor

3.8 Turn RIGHT on Coyote Point Drive.

4.1 End of the road at parking lot. Continue past lot onto levee.

4.3 End of bikeway on levee. Return back to yacht harbor area.

4.6 Turn RIGHT off road to get back on bikeway at Eucalyptus Grove Picnic Area. Bikeway goes around picnic area and then runs parallel to road, on the left.

5.0 Animal shelter on the right.

5.1 Turn RIGHT onto road.

5.3 Turn LEFT at the end of the road to get back on bikeway.

5.5 Beach center on the left.

5.9 Turn RIGHT onto Airport Boulevard.

6.1 Stay on road as it makes sharp left turn.

6.5 Turn RIGHT onto Bayview Place toward restaurant.

6.7 Get on bikeway on the far side of the restaurant and cross over wooden bridge. Then bear RIGHT to stay on bikeway along shoreline.

6.9 Sterling Suites Hotel on the left. Turn around and return the way you came.

12.6 Turn RIGHT off bikeway onto Mariners Island Boulevard. You must walk your bike across Third Avenue in the pedestrian crosswalk at this point, since there is no direct path to ride.

13.5 Back at the starting point.

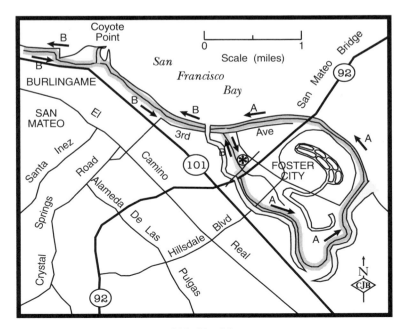

Ride No. 11

12 Woodside

Purisima Creek Redwoods Open Space Preserve

Region: Mid-Peninsula
Total Distance: 9 miles
Total Elevation Gain: 1600 feet
Type of Bike: Mountain Bike

Ride Rating: Difficult
Riding Time: 1-2 hours
Calories Burned: 1000

Terrain

Most of the ride is on dirt fire roads through the preserve. Some very steep sections may require you to walk your bike a small amount.

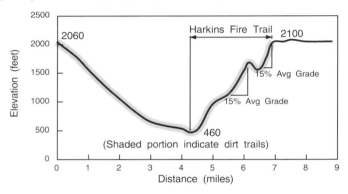

Ride Description

The headwaters for Purisima Creek form on the upper reaches of the western slope of the Santa Cruz Mountains. Following a path through lush redwood forests, the creek works its way to the ocean at a point about 4 miles south of Half Moon Bay. The Purisima Creek Open Space Preserve consists of about 2,500 acres of magnificent public land, open for the use of hikers, runners, equestrians, and bicyclists.

This ride encompasses nearly the entire preserve and allows the cyclist to experience the full range of pristine beauty available there. The ride begins with a steady descent through redwood forests, followed by a flat section along Purisima Creek and includes bridge crossings over the creek in several places. The return to the top of the mountain ridge is along Harkins Fire Trail. Although very steep in some places, this route affords some spectacular views of Half Moon Bay to the coast in the west. Once back at Skyline Boulevard, the return to the starting point is along a relatively flat section of Skyline Boulevard.

Starting Point

Begin the ride at the Purisima Creek trailhead, located about ½-mile from the intersection of Skyline Boulevard and Kings Mountain Road, above the town of Woodside. To get there, take the Woodside Road (Highway 84) exit from Highway 280 and proceed west toward Woodside. Continue through Woodside and turn right on Kings Mountain Road, following it all the way to the top, at Skyline Boulevard. Turn right on Skyline Boulevard and look for the Purisima Creek trailhead on the left side.

Ride Details and Mile Markers

0.0   From the trailhead, enter the park and follow Redwood Trail toward Purisima Creek Trail.

0.1   Turn LEFT onto Purisima Creek Trail.

1.9   Hikers-only trail intersection on the right side.

2.1   Trail follows along Purisima Creek.

2.3   Cross wooden bridge.

2.9   Grabtown Gulch Trail intersection on the left.

3.0   Cross second wooden bridge.

3.3   Borden Hatch Mill Trail intersection on the left.

4.2   Turn RIGHT onto Harkins Ridge Trail, cross bridge and then turn RIGHT again to stay on Harkins Ridge Trail.

5.1   Steep uphill section.

5.5   Another steep uphill section.

5.8   Soda Gulch Trail intersection on the right.

6.1   Bear LEFT to stay on trail and begin single-track. Views of Half Moon Bay on the left.

6.6   Turn RIGHT toward Skyline parking. Steep uphill.

6.8   Exit preserve and turn RIGHT onto Skyline Boulevard.

8.0   Mountain House restaurant on the right.

8.8   Back at the start point.

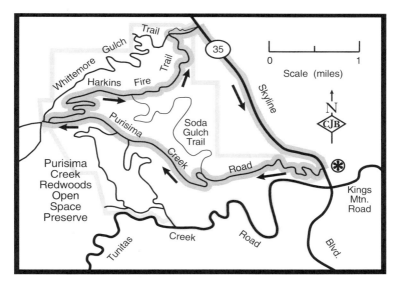

Ride No. 12

View from Harkins Fire Trail

Along the Pacific Coast
and on the Western Slope

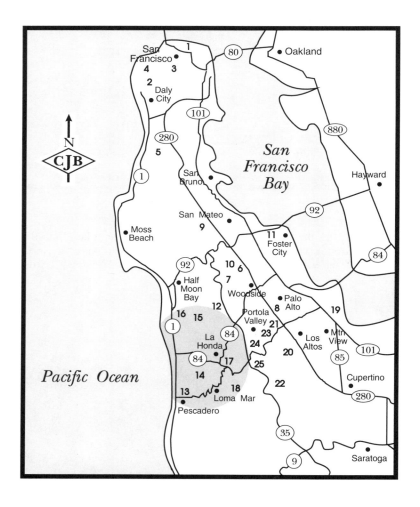

13 Pescadero
A Trio of Rides Around Pescadero

	Ride 13A	Ride 13B	Ride 13C
Region:	*Along the Pacific Coast*		
Ride Rating:	*Easy*	*Easy*	*Moderate*
Total Distance:	*17 miles*	*14 miles*	*29 miles*
Riding Time:	*1-2 hours*	*1-2 hours*	*3-4 hours*
Total Elevation Gain:	*1100 feet*	*500 feet*	*1400 feet*
Calories Burned:	*600*	*500*	*900*
Type of Bike:	*Road Bike*	*Road Bike*	*Road Bike*

Ride Description

Pescadero is a small agricultural town directly west of Woodside and about two miles inland from the coast. Its quaint country charm is enhanced by several notable restaurants, antique shops and small churches.

Just outside of town, at the intersection of Pescadero Road and Highway 1, lies the Pescadero Marsh Natural Preserve, a key link in a chain of coastal wetlands stretching along the western coast of North America. The wetlands serve as home to many species of birds, mammals, and fishes, and provide for essential resting places for the many migratory birds in their travels north and south on the coast. There are hiking trails through the marsh and observation points for viewing the resident and transient wildlife.

Along Highway 1, south of Pescadero, lies the Pigeon Point Lighthouse and youth hostel. Beaming its beacon to offshore vessels for more than 100 years, this lighthouse is probably the most photographed of all on the west coast. Occasionally you may find a Coast Guard representative present at the lighthouse to give you a brief tour of the structure.

Starting Point

Start each of the rides in the town of Pescadero, located on the coast about 16 miles south of Half Moon Bay. To get to Pescadero, take the Woodside Road (Highway 84) exit off of Interstate Highway 280 and follow Woodside Road west through Woodside, over the mountain, and down into La Honda. Turn left just past La Honda on Pescadero Road and follow it all the way to Pescadero. Park anywhere around town and begin the ride at the intersection of Pescadero Road and Stage Road.

Ride 13A (Easy)

This ride consists of a loop north of Pescadero toward San Gregorio on Stage Road, a lightly traveled eucalyptus-lined road formerly used as the main stagecoach route before the completion of Highway 1. The southward return to Pescadero is along Highway 1, with stunning views of the rugged California coastline.

Terrain

Stage Road is a lightly traveled country road with several hills of about 300 feet in elevation. Highway 1 on the coast is relatively flat and will normally provide you with a friendly tailwind.

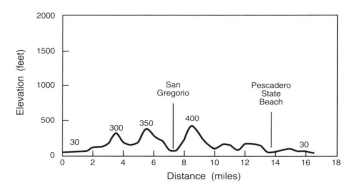

Ride 13A: Ride Details and Mile Markers

- 0.0   From Pescadero, head NORTH out of town on Stage Road, away from Pescadero Road.
- 4.8   Pomponio Road intersection on the right.
- 7.5   Continue STRAIGHT at intersection with Highway 84 (La Honda Road.
- 8.6   Turn LEFT onto Highway 1.
- 9.9   Continue STRAIGHT at intersection with Highway 84, on the left. San Gregorio State Beach on the right.
- 11.7   Pomponio State Beach on the right.
- 14.6   Turn LEFT onto Pescadero Road. Pescadero State Beach on the right.
- 16.0   Bean Hollow Road intersection on the right.
- 16.6   Back at Pescadero.

Ride 13B (Easy)

Ride 13B proceeds south from Pescadero along Bean Hollow Road and then Highway 1, past the Pigeon Point Lighthouse, and returns along inland roads, Gazos Creek Road and Cloverdale Road. The inland stretch also passes by Butano State Park, which contains hiking trails through majestic coastal redwoods and fern-lined stream beds.

Terrain

You will have little or no traffic on Bean Hollow Road, but will experience a substantial number of cars on Highway 1. A brisk tailwind and an adequate shoulder on Highway 1 will permit you to speedily cover the miles to Gazos Creek Road, along which you will again experience little traffic. Moderately hilly terrain and some headwinds on Cloverdale Road will give you occasional challenge.

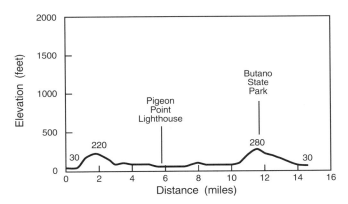

Ride 13B: Ride Details and Mile Markers

0.0   From Pescadero, head WEST on Pescadero Road toward the ocean.

0.6   Turn LEFT onto Bean Hollow Road.

3.0   Turn LEFT onto Highway 1.

5.8   Pigeon Point Lighthouse on the right side.

8.1   Turn LEFT onto Gazos Creek Road. Gazos Creek State Beach on the right.

10.2   Begin Cloverdale Road at point where road makes a sharp left turn.

11.5   Butano State Park on the right.

12.5   Canyon Road intersection on the right.

13.8   Turn LEFT onto Pescadero Road.

14.4   Back at Pescadero.

Ride 13C (Moderate)

This ride combines rides 13A and 13B into a single loop. Initially going north out of Pescadero to San Gregorio, the route returns southward along Highway 1 on the coast and continues past Pescadero to the Pigeon Point Lighthouse, about 5 miles south of Pescadero. Just beyond the lighthouse, the route heads inland along Gazos Creek Road and returns to Pescadero along Cloverdale Road.

Terrain

Country roads with some small hills along and little or no car traffic combine with busy Highway 1 with its prevailing tailwinds to give you a lot of riding variety on this ride.

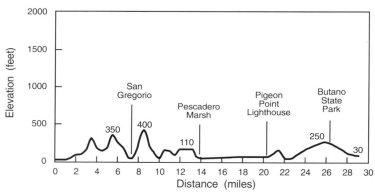

Ride 13C: Ride Details and Mile Markers

0.0 From Pescadero, head NORTH out of town on Stage Road, away from Pescadero Road.

4.8 Pomponio Road intersection on the right.

7.5 Continue STRAIGHT at intersection with Highway 84 (La Honda Road.

8.6 Turn LEFT onto Highway 1.

9.9 Continue STRAIGHT at intersection with Highway 84, on the left. San Gregorio State Beach on the right.

11.7 Pomponio State Beach on the right.

14.6 Continue STRAIGHT at intersection with Pescadero Road, on the left. Pescadero State Beach on the right.

17.5 Bean Hollow Road intersection on the left.

20.3 Pigeon Point Lighthouse on the right side.

22.6 Turn LEFT onto Gazos Creek Road. Gazos Creek State Beach on the right.

24.7 Begin Cloverdale Road at point where road makes a sharp left turn.

26.0 Butano State Park on the right.

27.0   Canyon Road intersection on the right.

28.3   Turn LEFT onto Pescadero Road.

28.9   Back at Pescadero.

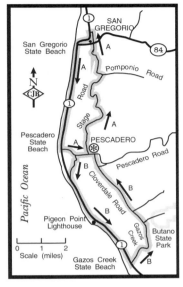

Rides No. 13A and 13B   Ride No. 13C

Pigeon Point Lighthouse

14 Pescadero

Pescadero — La Honda — San Gregorio Loop

Region: *Along the Pacific Coast*
Total Distance: *28 miles*
Total Elevation Gain: *1500 feet*
Type of Bike: *Road Bike*

Ride Rating: *Moderate*
Riding Time: *3-4 hours*
Calories Burned: *900*

Terrain

This ride features country roads with generally very light car traffic, with the exception of about 7 miles on La Honda Road (Highway 84), where you will encounter some traffic but will have a wide shoulder for safety. The terrain is moderately hilly with one substantial climb to about 1000 feet above sea level.

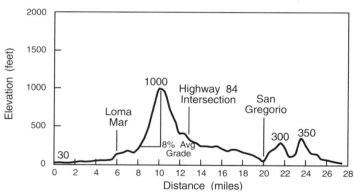

Ride Description

This loop on the western slope of the Santa Cruz Mountains takes you through three small towns: Pescadero, La Honda, and San Gregorio, each with its own flavor and personality.

Pescadero, the starting point, is the largest of the three towns, but still retains the small town charms that have characterized the community for over 100 years. Antique shops and quaint churches give the town a close resemblance to those in rural New England. Once out of town, however, the resemblance ends as the hillsides and farmlands remind you of the uniqueness that is Northern California. Pescadero Road takes you east out of town and follows Pescadero Creek, first along farmlands and then through dense redwood forests, passing the hamlet of Loma Mar and San Mateo County Memorial Park and then climbing to an elevation of about 1000 feet to cross Haskins Ridge. From the summit you can view the Butano Forest in the distance toward the south. The steep descent through the shady forest brings you into La Honda.

The second town in the loop, La Honda, stands in stark contrast to Pescadero by virtue of its location deep in the redwoods of the mountain foothills. Home to residents seeking isolation from the hustle and bustle of the modern world, yet still retaining the friendliness of former times, La Honda is a world in itself. Heading west on La Honda Road, you follow San Gregorio Creek slightly downhill, but with a headwind stiff enough to force you to pedal. After passing farmlands rich with artichokes and other produce, you wind up in San Gregorio, the smallest of the three towns, and home to one of its most unique places, the Peterson and Alsford General Store, at the intersection of La Honda Road and Stage Road.

Over 100 years old, the store supplies a vast array of merchandise and services, and most notably serves as a popular local gathering place and a favorite rest stop for cyclists enjoying the country roads in the area. Proceeding south from San Gregorio on Stage Road, you cross two modest hills, each of about 400 feet above sea level, through several picturesque and aromatic eucalyptus groves, and past charming farms and ranches on your way back into Pescadero.

Ranch near Pescadero on Stage Road

Starting Point

Start the ride in Pescadero, where there are several interesting stores and restaurants worth visiting after your ride. To get there, take the Woodside Road (Highway 84) exit off of Interstate Highway 280 and follow Woodside Road through Woodside, over the mountain, and down into La Honda. Turn left just past La Honda on Pescadero Road and follow it all the way to Pescadero. Park anywhere around town and begin the ride at the intersection of Pescadero Road and Stage Road.

Ride Details and Mile Markers

0.0 From Pescadero, head EAST out of town on Pescadero Road.

0.6 Cloverdale Road intersection on the right.

1.4 Butano Cut-off intersection on the right.

6.1 Loma Mar store on the right.

7.4 San Mateo County Memorial Park headquarters on the right.

7.9 Begin uphill section.

9.9 Summit — 1000 feet.

11.6 Bear LEFT at intersection with Alpine Road.

12.8 Turn LEFT onto Highway 84 (La Honda Road).

18.2 Bear Gulch Road intersection on the right.

20.1 Turn LEFT onto Stage Road. The Peterson and Alsford Store (on the right) is a good place to stop for a break.

21.9 First summit — 300 feet.

23.7 Second summit — 350 feet. Begin descent toward Pescadero.

27.4 Back at Pescadero.

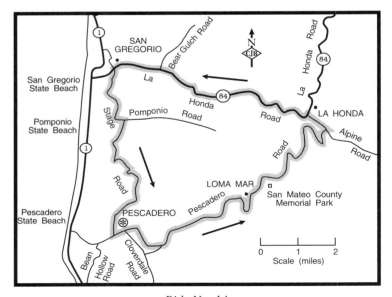

Ride No. 14

15 Half Moon Bay
Tunitas Creek Road

Region: *Along the Pacific Coast* **Ride Rating:** *Difficult*
Total Distance: *29 miles* **Riding Time:** *3-4 hours*
Total Elevation Gain: *2200 feet* **Calories Burned:** *1100*
Type of Bike: *Road Bike*

Terrain

The ride is mostly along country roads, except for 6 miles on Skyline Boulevard, 4 miles on busy Highway 92, and a short distance on Highway 1 on the coast. There is a 4-mile unpaved stretch on Lobitas Creek Road, but it is easily passable with road bike tires. A long and steady 6% hill climb on traffic-free Tunitas Creek Road through dense redwood forests provides plenty of challenge for those who like hills.

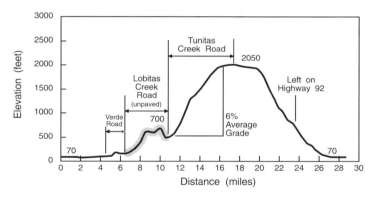

Ride Description

Half Moon Bay is a delightful seaside resort community, serving both San Francisco and the Santa Clara Valley. Its frequent annual events include a Portuguese Festival in the spring and the famous Pumpkin festival in the fall. The Clam Chowder and Chili Cook-Off and the annual Harbor Day, both in the summer, are events also worth attending.

This ride is a challenging one by virtue of the climb on Tunitas Creek Road and includes a wide variety of scenery and terrain. Proceeding south from downtown Half Moon Bay for a short distance on Highway 1, the route takes you quickly inland along rolling and scenic Verde Road, past fields and pastureland devoid of car traffic. A 4-mile passage on Lobitas Creek Road offers the rare chance to ride on an unpaved, but completely passable, road through more rural countryside on the way to Tunitas Creek Road.

Ideally suited for cyclists, Tunitas Creek Road takes you up a long and gradual climb through dense redwood forests with little or no car traffic. The frequent coastal fog at the lower elevations adds a surrealistic feeling to the natural beauty of this, one of the most delightful, cycling roads on the Peninsula. Following along Tunitas Creek, you can experience the tranquility of the lush forests which were once aggressively harvested to supply building materials for the growing Bay Area.

At the top, you follow Skyline Boulevard north along the ridge of the mountains. As you descend toward Highway 92, you will usually be able to experience some spectacular views of both the Santa Clara Valley to the east, and the Pacific Coast to the west.

On Highway 92, to head back to Half Moon Bay, you will encounter the heaviest traffic on the ride. Riding downhill into town will get you there quickly, however, and you can often even keep up with the cars. You should be extra careful, nevertheless, to stay as far to the right on the road surface as you can, and keep your hands on your brakes. Once back into Half Moon Bay, be sure to browse around the town and reward yourself with a meal or refreshment at one of the many delightful eating establishments there.

Starting Point

The ride starts in downtown Half Moon Bay, at the intersection of State Highway 92 (Half Moon Bay Road) and Main Street. To get there, take the Highway 92 exit from Interstate Highway 280 and head west towards Half Moon Bay. Continue until just before you reach the end of Highway 92 at its intersection with Highway 1. There are many places to park near this intersection.

Ride Details and Mile Markers

0.0   From Half Moon Bay, head SOUTH on Main Street, going directly through town.

1.3   Turn LEFT onto Highway 1, heading south.

4.5   Turn LEFT onto Verde Road. (Note that this is the first of three places where Verde Road is accessible from Highway 1).

4.9   Bear RIGHT to stay on Verde Road (Purisima Creek Road intersects on the left).

6.3   Continue STRAIGHT at Verde Road access spur to Highway 1 on the right.

6.5   Turn LEFT onto Lobitas Creek Road. This is a dirt road, but is passable with a road bike.

10.7   Turn LEFT onto Tunitas Creek Road.

15.3 Star Hill Road intersection on the right.

16.6 Turn LEFT onto Skyline Blvd (top of the hill).

17.7 Kings Mountain Fire Station on the right. Emergency telephone available.

17.9 Mountain House Restaurant on the left.

19.2 Purisima Creek Redwoods Open Space Preserve on the left.

19.3 Kings Mountain Store on the left.

23.6 Turn LEFT onto Highway 92 (Half Moon Bay Road).

25.4 Cross Pilarcitos Creek.

26.9 Obester Winery and tasting room on the left.

28.6 Back at Main Street intersection in Half Moon Bay.

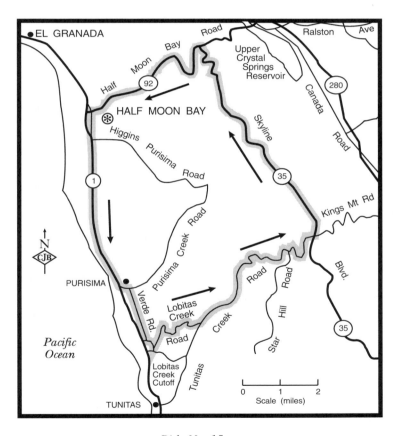

Ride No. 15

16 Half Moon Bay
Half Moon Bay and Purisima Creek

	Ride 16A	Ride 16B
Region:	*Along the Pacific Coast*	
Ride Rating:	*Easy*	*Moderate*
Total Distance:	*14 miles*	*23 miles*
Riding Time:	*1-2 hours*	*2-3 hours*
Total Elevation Gain:	*550 feet*	*900 feet*
Calories Burned:	*400*	*700*
Type of Bike:	*Road Bike*	*Road Bike*

Ride Description

The coastal resort town of Half Moon Bay has served as a respite from the hectic lifestyles of Peninsula residents for many years. So near to the urban centers and suburban sprawl of the Bay Area, it still seems like another world—a perfect place to unwind for a weekend. The numerous hotels and restaurants of the area, as well as the many diverse annual events and festivals, beckon the outsider to come to visit.

Starting Point

The ride starts in downtown Half Moon Bay. To get there, take the Highway 92 exit from Interstate Highway 280 and head west towards Half Moon Bay. Continue until you reach Main Street, just before the end of Highway 92 at its intersection with Highway 1. Park somewhere near downtown and start the ride at the corner of Main Street and Kelly Avenue.

Ride 16A (Easy)

Ride 16A, the easiest of the two rides, takes you south out of town along Highway 1 for about 4 miles, where you proceed inland along Verde Road and then Purisima Creek Road. Here you will find little or no car traffic. Passing rural ranches and pastureland, you reach one of the major trail heads for Purisima Creek Open Space Preserve, in which hikers, cyclists, and equestrians experience the peace and tranquility of lush forest trails. A moderate climb of about 600 feet elevation gain rewards you with views west toward the valley below and the coast beyond. After you descend along Higgins Purisima Road and approach the highway ahead, be sure to look to your left for a prominent white house in an open area. The James Johnston House, listed on the National Register for Historic Places, dates from 1855 and copies the style of the original Johnston family home in Ohio.

Terrain

There is some travel on busy Highway 1, flat with a usual tailwind. The inland roads are lightly traveled rolling rural roads with one hill climb with an elevation of about 600 feet.

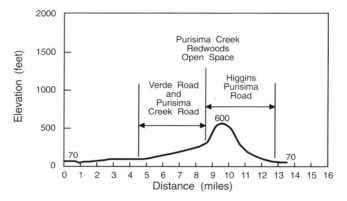

Ride 16A: Ride Details and Mile Markers

0.0   From Half Moon Bay, head SOUTH on Main Street, going directly through town.

1.0   Turn LEFT onto Highway 1, heading south.

4.2   Turn left onto Verde Road. (Note that this is the first of three places where Verde Road is accessible from Highway 1).

4.6   Bear LEFT onto Purisima Creek Road.

7.8   Cross bridge.

8.3   Purisima Creek Redwoods Open Space Preserve on the right. Begin Higgins Purisima Road at the hairpin turn.

9.3   Summit — 600 feet.

12.6   Turn RIGHT onto Main Street (just before Highway 1).

13.6   Back at downtown Half Moon Bay.

Ride 16B (Moderate)

Ride 16B adds a loop onto Ride 16A, taking you south on Highway 1 past Verde Road to Tunitas Creek Road. You head inland at Tunitas Creek Road and return to Purisima Creek Road by way of an inland route past remote farms and ranches. Once on Purisima Creek Road, the ride back to Half Moon Bay is identical to Ride 16A and passes both Purisima Creek Open Space Preserve and the Johnston House.

Terrain

Like Ride 16A, this route follows Highway 1, generally flat with a tailwind. The inland roads have little or no car traffic with one 600-foot hill to climb.

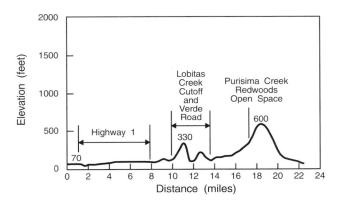

Ride 16B: Ride Details and Mile Markers

0.0 From Half Moon Bay, head SOUTH on Main Street, going directly through town.

1.0 Turn LEFT onto Highway 1, heading south.

4.2 First Verde Road intersection on the left.

5.8 Second Verde Road intersection on the left.

6.1 Third Verde Road intersection on the left.

7.8 Turn LEFT onto Tunitas Creek Road.

9.9 Turn LEFT onto Lobitas Creek Cutoff.

11.6 Turn RIGHT onto Verde Road.

11.7 Lobitas Creek Road intersection on the right.

11.9 Verde Road access spur to Highway 1 on the left.

13.5 Turn RIGHT onto Purisima Creek Road.

17.2 Purisima Creek Redwoods Open Space Preserve on the right. Begin Higgins Purisima Road at the hairpin turn.

18.2 Summit — 600 feet.

21.5 Turn RIGHT onto Main Street (just before Highway 1).

22.5 Back at downtown Half Moon Bay.

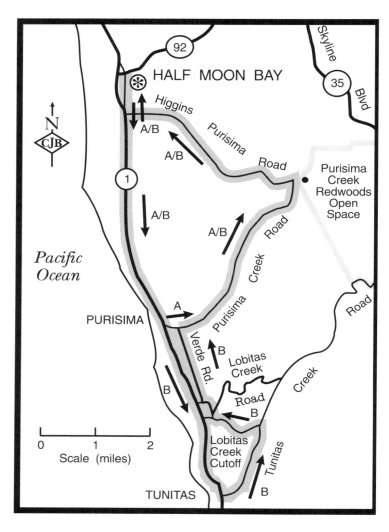

Ride No. 16

17 La Honda
La Honda — Alpine Road — Skyline Blvd Loop

Region: *Along the Pacific Coast*	**Ride Rating:** *Difficult*
Total Distance: *21 miles*	**Riding Time:** *3 hours*
Total Elevation Gain: *1900 feet*	**Calories Burned:** *900*
Type of Bike: *Road Bike*	

Terrain

The roads are all well-paved, but may have some car traffic to contend with, at least on Skyline Boulevard and La Honda Road. Each has a sufficient shoulder, however, to provide an adequate safety margin. On the other hand, Alpine Road has a very small shoulder, but the lack of car traffic compensates somewhat.

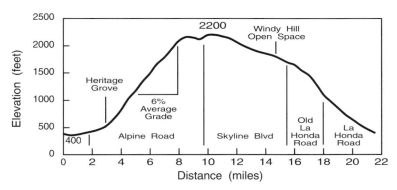

Ride Description

The village of La Honda stands out in dramatic contrast to the densely populated cities and towns of the Greater Bay Area. Nestled in the forests in the western foothills of the Santa Cruz Mountains, La Honda presents an aura of an old-fashioned mountain town. Damp, dark, and rustic, it often provides a very pleasant respite from sweltering heat that sometimes invades inland flatlands.

Starting from La Honda, the route takes you along a flat section of Pescadero Road past Sam McDonald County Park, to intersect Alpine Road. At Alpine Road, the main climb begins, gaining about 1800 feet over 8 miles. In the steep sections, the grade averages about 6%. The climb, through thick redwood forests, passes directly by Heritage Grove, part of the San Mateo County Park System, containing trails through the woods along Alpine Creek and connecting to Pescadero County Park.

At the top of the climb, at Skyline Boulevard, you climb a little more and then begin a steady descent all the way back to La Honda. Panoramic vistas of the Santa Clara Valley to the east will delight you on clear days, as will the views to the west, stretching all the way to the coast. The connection to Old La Honda Road comes suddenly on Skyline Boulevard, so you should be careful not to miss the turn. Old La Honda Road carries very little car traffic and allows you to savor the experience of true country road riding as you descend to get to La Honda Road (Highway 84) for the final return back into La Honda.

Starting Point

The ride starts in La Honda. To get to there, take the Woodside Road (Highway 84) exit off of Interstate Highway 280 and follow Woodside Road west through Woodside, over the mountain, and down into La Honda. There is a small grocery store on the right side with public parking.

Ride Details and Mile Markers

0.0 Proceed WEST on Highway 84 (La Honda Road), heading toward the coast.

0.6 Turn LEFT onto Pescadero Road.

1.7 Turn LEFT onto Alpine Road.

3.0 Heritage Grove Redwoods Preserve on the right side.

4.5 Alpine Ranch on the right side.

5.5 Intersection for Pescadero Creek County Park on the right side.

5.9 Bear LEFT at the stop sign to stay on Alpine Road. Portola State Park is down the road to the right.

9.4 Russian Ridge Open Space Preserve on the left side.

9.5 Turn LEFT onto Highway 35 (Skyline Boulevard).

10.6 Vista Point on the right side.

14.5 Windy Hill Open Space Preserve on the right side.

15.4 Turn LEFT onto Old La Honda Road.

18.0 Turn LEFT onto Highway 84 (La Honda Road).

21.3 Back at La Honda center.

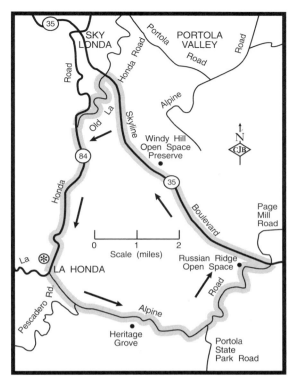

Ride No. 17

Pastoral scene along Alpine Road

18　Loma Mar
Old Haul Road

	Ride 18A	Ride 18B
Region:	Along the Pacific Coast	
Ride Rating:	Moderate	Difficult
Total Distance:	16 miles	21 miles
Riding Time:	2 hours	3-4 hours
Total Elevation Gain:	800 feet	2200 feet
Calories Burned:	700	1000
Type of Bike:	Mountain Bike	Mountain Bike

Ride Description

The lumber demand created by the California Gold Rush of 1849 was met by the seemingly endless redwood forests of the Santa Cruz Mountains. Getting the timber out of the forests, however, required the construction of roads and railways. One of these, no longer in use for lumber harvesting, is today called Old Haul Road, and is located within Pescadero Creek County Park. Following a route through the park, it extends from Loma Mar, just east of Pescadero, to Portola State Park. A recreational trail for use by hikers, cyclists and equestrians, Old Haul Road, by virtue of its former use as a railroad bed, does not present the extreme steep terrain usually associated with off-road cycling. With the exception of a few short steep sections, the grade is a gentle one and the trails are all very well-marked.

The first known settler after the Gold Rush was a Scandinavian named Christian Iverson, who built a small cabin in what is today Portola State Park. The remains of the cabin are still present. After Iverson, the land passed through the hands of several owners before it was acquired by the State of California and subsequently established as a park in 1945.

Starting Point

Start the ride in Loma Mar, about 6 miles east of Pescadero, at the Loma Mar Store. To get there, take the Woodside Road (Highway 84) exit off of Interstate Highway 280 and follow Woodside Road through Woodside, over the mountain, and down into La Honda. Turn left just past La Honda on Pescadero Road and follow it all the way to Loma Mar. The Loma Mar Store is the only public structure in Loma Mar, which would be easy to miss were it not for the store. Park anywhere nearby and begin the ride at the store.

Ride 18A (Moderate)

Ride 18A, the easier of the two rides, takes you from Loma Mar into Pescadero Creek County Park and along Old Haul Road to the park headquarters of Portola State Park. The return is along the same route.

Terrain

Old Haul Road, the focus of Ride 18A, is a wide trail on a gentle grade, with only a few steep sections, none very long.

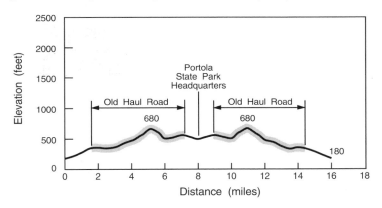

Ride 18A: Ride Details and Mile Markers

0.0 From the Loma Mar Store, head EAST on Pescadero Road.

0.1 Turn RIGHT onto Wurr Road.

1.6 Turn RIGHT into Pescadero County Park onto Old Haul Road and continue past the entrance gate onto the dirt road.

2.2 Continue past the gate.

2.4 Pomponio Trail intersection on the left.

3.0 Towne Trail intersection on the left.

3.5 Butano Ridge Loop Trail intersection on the right.

5.2 Crest — 680 feet elevation.

5.9 Bridge Trail intersection on the left.

6.0 Butano Ridge Loop Trail intersection on the right.

7.1 Turn LEFT off Old Haul Road at the entrance to Portola State Park. Begin steep descent for short distance.

7.2 Continue past the gate and onto the paved road. Iverson cabin site is on the right side of the trail just before the gate.

7.4 Park service area on the left.

8.0 Portola State Park headquarters and public restrooms. Return back on the road the way you came.

8.8 Gate and Iverson cabin site.

8.9 Turn RIGHT to get back onto Old Haul Road.

10.1 Bridge Trail intersection on the right.

10.8 Crest of the hill.

13.0 Towne Trail intersection on the right.

13.8 Continue past the gate.

14.4 Turn LEFT to get back onto Wurr Road.

15.9 Turn LEFT onto Pescadero Road.

16.0 Back at Loma Mar Store.

Ride 18B (Difficult)

For a little more difficulty and variety, Ride 18B not only follows Old Haul Road to Portola State Park, but continues through the park and climbs paved Portola State Park Road to Alpine Road. Alpine Road winds downhill toward La Honda, passing Heritage Grove, a stand of old-growth redwoods. A second climb along Pescadero Road takes you through even more forests as it climbs over Haskins Ridge and then descends to return you to Loma Mar.

Terrain

Ride 18B includes a 1000-foot climb on Portola State Park Road, a 4-mile descent on Alpine Road, and a 600-foot climb on Pescadero Road. All surface roads carry little car traffic, but are narrow with small shoulders.

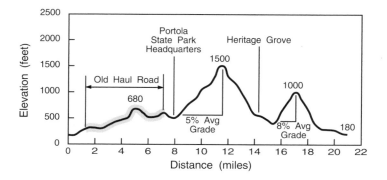

Ride 18B: Ride Details and Mile Markers

0.0   From the Loma Mar Store, head EAST on Pescadero Road.

0.1   Turn RIGHT onto Wurr Road.

1.6   Turn RIGHT into Pescadero County Park onto Old Haul Road and continue past the entrance gate onto the dirt road.

2.2   Continue past the gate.

2.4   Pomponio Trail intersection on the left.

3.0   Towne Trail intersection on the left.

3.5   Butano Ridge Loop Trail intersection on the right.

5.2   Crest — 680 feet elevation.

5.9   Bridge Trail intersection on the left.

6.0   Butano Ridge Loop Trail intersection on the right.

7.1   Turn LEFT off Old Haul Road at the entrance to Portola State Park. Begin steep descent for short distance.

7.2   Continue past the gate and onto the paved road. Iverson cabin site is on the right side of the trail just before the gate.

7.4   Park service area on the left.

8.0   Portola State Park headquarters and public restrooms on the left.

8.5   Portola State Park entrance and exit.

11.5 Turn LEFT onto Alpine Road.

11.9 Bear RIGHT at Camp Pomponio Road intersection to stay on Alpine Road.

IVERSON CABIN

Courtesy of Santa Cruz Mountains Natural History Association

14.3 Heritage Grove on left.
15.6 Turn LEFT onto Pescadero Road.
16.1 Sam McDonald County Park on the right.
16.9 Crest — 1000 feet.
19.8 San Mateo County Memorial Park entrance on the left.
21.1 Back at Loma Mar Store.

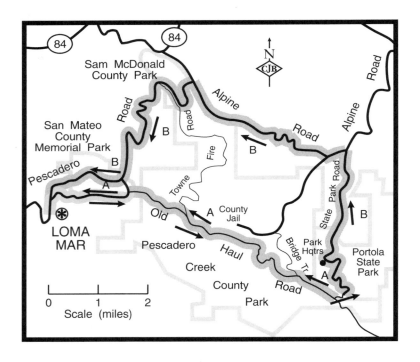

Ride No. 18

Palo Alto
and the Lower Peninsula

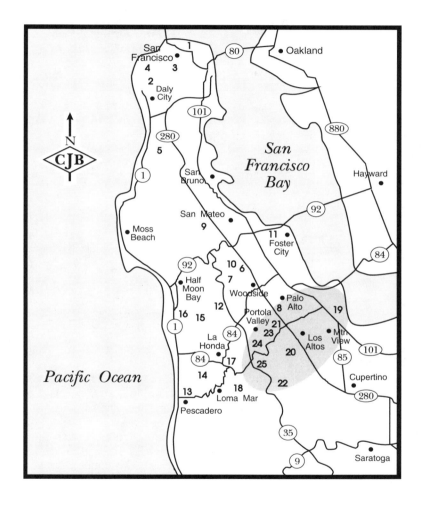

19   Palo Alto
Stanford University and Shoreline Park

Region: *Lower Peninsula*
Total Distance: *20 miles*
Total Elevation Gain: *40 feet*
Type of Bike: *Road Bike*

Ride Rating: *Easy*
Riding Time: *2-3 hours*
Calories Burned: *400*

Terrain

This is a completely flat ride, with the exception of some highway overpasses. The route follows surface streets in Palo Alto with wide bike lanes, and then paved and gravel paths through Shoreline Park. Some muddy sections may be encountered after a recent rain.

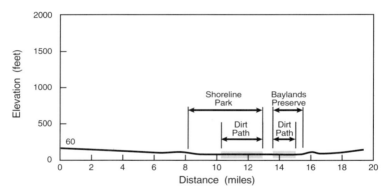

Ride Description

Starting on the Stanford University campus, this route takes you through the tree-lined residential areas of fashionable Palo Alto to Mountain View and its Shoreline Park. Built on reclaimed land using modern landfill techniques, Shoreline Park includes a municipal golf course, a sailing lake and the Shoreline Amphitheater, an outdoor stage for world-class entertainment shows. Trails through the park offer rare glimpses of nesting and migrating birds, as well as stunning views of San Francisco Bay. Walkers, runners, and cyclists share the trails, so be sure to be extra cautious and courteous at all times.

Just north of Shoreline Park is the Palo Alto Baylands Preserve, with similar trails leading around the periphery of Palo Alto Municipal Airport through more wetlands. The return to the campus is again through Palo Alto's residential neighborhoods and downtown Palo

Alto, where you will find a wide assortment of interesting restaurants and refreshments awaiting you.

Starting Point

Begin the ride at the Stanford University campus in Palo Alto near the football stadium. To get there, take Highway 101 to the exit for Embarcadero Road. Follow Embarcadero Road across El Camino Real onto the Stanford campus. Embarcadero Road becomes Galvez Street after crossing El Camino Real. Plenty of parking is usually available between the stadium and the Sport Shop, on Galvez Street.

Ride Details and Mile Markers

0.0   From the stadium parking lot, turn LEFT onto Galvez Street, heading toward the middle of the campus.

0.1   Turn LEFT onto East Campus Drive.

0.5   Turn LEFT onto Serra Street.

1.0   Turn LEFT onto El Camino Real.

1.2   Turn RIGHT onto Churchill Avenue.

1.8   Turn RIGHT onto Waverley Street, LEFT onto Coleridge Avenue and RIGHT onto Cowper Street.

2.7   Cross Oregon Expressway.

3.4   Turn LEFT onto Loma Verde Avenue.

3.5   Turn RIGHT onto Middlefield Road.

5.2   Bear RIGHT to stay on Middlefield Road.

6.7   Turn LEFT onto Shoreline Boulevard.

8.2   Enter Shoreline Park on Shoreline Boulevard. Follow the bike path along the right side of the road.

9.2   Turn RIGHT on bike path just after you cross footbridge.

9.3   Turn RIGHT again almost immediately.

10.0   Bear RIGHT at trail split.

10.3   Turn RIGHT to head out onto a dirt trail on levee.

12.3   Cross over flood control dam.

12.5   Gate at the end of the bike path.

12.9   Turn RIGHT onto the road.

13.1   Continue straight at Embarcadero Road intersection.

13.2   Palo Alto airport on the left.

13.3   Duck pond on the left.

13.6   Turn LEFT on the gravel bike path just beyond the airport to enter the Palo Alto Baylands Preserve.

13.6   Lucy Evans Baylands Nature Interpretive Center on the right.

13.9   Go past gate and turn RIGHT to stay on the dirt path. Continue around the airport and past the golf course.

14.8   Continue past gate and bear LEFT.

15.4 Bear LEFT to get off the bike path and head toward the parking lot.

15.6 Continue straight through the parking lot at the end of the bike path.

15.7 Turn RIGHT onto Embarcadero Road.

16.0 Cross over Highway 101 overpass.

16.2 Turn RIGHT onto St. Francis

16.3 Turn LEFT onto Channing Avenue.

17.6 Turn RIGHT onto Gunda Street.

17.7 Turn LEFT onto Homer Avenue.

18.2 Turn RIGHT onto Waverley Avenue.

18.4 Turn LEFT onto University Avenue.

18.9 Cross El Camino Real and enter the university on Palm Drive.

19.2 Turn LEFT onto Arboretum Road.

19.5 Turn RIGHT onto Galvez Street.

19.7 Back at the stadium.

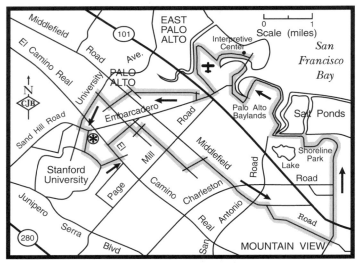

Ride No. 19

20   Los Altos
Tour of the Los Altos Hills

Region: *Lower Peninsula*	**Ride Rating:** *Easy*
Total Distance: *14 miles*	**Riding Time:** *2 hours*
Total Elevation Gain: *600 feet*	**Calories Burned:** *400*
Type of Bike: *Road Bike*	

Terrain

This ride, although rated as "Easy" because of its relatively short distance, has one moderate hill to climb. All the roads are well-paved and most have little traffic, except for Foothill Expressway, which has a wide shoulder to compensate.

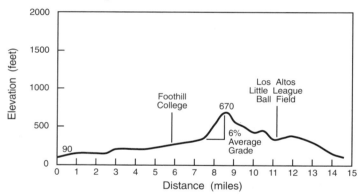

Ride Description

The town of Los Altos is a very pleasant place to start and end the ride, by virtue of its numerous restaurants and shops and its access to plenty of free parking.

The route begins by following busy Foothill Expressway south toward Cupertino. After about 2.5 miles, you will leave Foothill Expressway and enter the quiet residential neighborhoods of Los Altos Hills. Passing by Los Altos Hills Country Club, you continue past luxurious homes and do a complete loop around the small, but pleasant campus of Foothill College.

After climbing the hill on Altamont Road, you are rewarded with views of the Santa Clara Valley below you. Descending on Taaffe Road, you will pass by picturesque orchards, especially beautiful with springtime mustard grass blooming. The return to downtown Los Altos takes you by homes with riding stables and little league ballfields.

Starting Point

Start the ride in downtown Los Altos. There is ample parking in the parking lot in the rear of the stores on Main Street. To get there, take Interstate Highway 280 to the El Monte Road exit and head east on El Monte toward Los Altos. Turn left on Foothill Expressway and follow it for about one mile to Main Street. Turn right on Main Street and park anywhere around town. Begin the ride at the corner of Main Street and Third Street.

Ride Details and Mile Markers

0.0   Proceed on Main Street toward Foothill Expressway.

0.2   Turn LEFT onto Foothill Expressway.

0.8   Continue STRAIGHT at El Monte Road intersection.

2.6   Turn RIGHT at Loyola Drive exit and turn RIGHT immediately.

2.7   Bear LEFT to go up the hill on Loyola Drive. There are several roads intersecting at this point, so be sure you get on Loyola Drive.

2.9   Los Altos Country Club on the right side.

3.3   Begin Fairway Drive.

3.8   Turn LEFT onto Hillview Drive.

4.0   Continue STRAIGHT at Magdalena Road intersection.

4.4   Turn RIGHT onto Hilltop Drive.

4.5   Turn LEFT onto Summerhill Avenue.

5.2   Turn LEFT onto El Monte Road.

5.6   Freeway underpass.

5.8   Turn RIGHT into Foothill College campus.

6.0   Turn RIGHT at stop sign (Perimeter Road) to go around campus.

6.9   Turn RIGHT at the stop sign to exit the campus. This will get you on Moody Road.

7.0   Bear LEFT onto Moody Road and begin to climb.

7.2   Turn RIGHT onto Altamont Road and continue climbing.

8.3   Turn RIGHT onto Taaffe Road at the crest of hill and begin descent.

9.2   Turn LEFT onto Elena Road.

11.0   Turn RIGHT onto Purissima Road.

11.2   Ball field on the right side.

11.7   Roble Ladera Road intersection on the left.

11.9   Turn LEFT onto Concepcion Road.

12.8   Turn RIGHT onto Fremont Road.

13.7   Turn LEFT onto Edith Avenue.

13.9   Cross Foothill Expressway.

14.2   Turn RIGHT onto Third Street.

14.4   Back at the starting point.

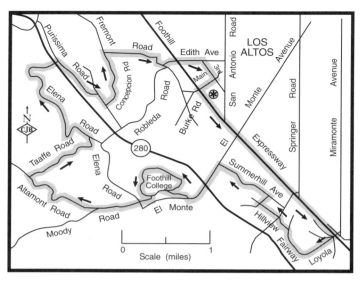

Ride No. 20

View from Altamont Road in Los Altos Hills

21 **Palo Alto**

Stanford University and Portola Valley Loop

	Ride 21A	Ride 21B
Region:	*Lower Peninsula*	
Ride Rating:	*Easy*	*Moderate*
Total Distance:	*13 miles*	*18 miles*
Riding Time:	*1-2 hours*	*2 hours*
Total Elevation Gain:	*370 feet*	*500 feet*
Calories Burned:	*300*	*450*
Type of Bike:	*Road Bike*	*Road Bike*

Ride Description

The Stanford University campus, affectionately referred to as "The Farm," was originally the property of Leland and Jane Stanford, and was, in fact, the Palo Alto Stock Farm, owned and operated by the Stanfords as a horse breeding ranch in the late 1800's. One of early California's most prominent citizens, Leland Stanford, gained his early fame and his fortune, as well as the head of the Central Pacific Railroad. Later, he became governor of California and then U.S. Senator, until his death in 1893.

The Stanford's only son, Leland, Jr., died of typhoid in 1884, at the age of 15. As a memorial to their beloved son, the Stanford's founded the university, using "The Farm" as the site for the campus. The property totals over 8,000 acres, all of which is prime California real estate stretching from the flatlands of the Santa Clara Valley up into the foothills of the Santa Cruz Mountains.

At the heart of the campus is the Inner Quadrangle, consisting of the twelve original classroom buildings and the Memorial Church. The architecture on campus, a blend of Romanesque and Mission Revival styles, was carefully designed to blend in harmoniously with the climate and landscape of Northern California.

Starting Point

The ride starts on the Stanford University campus in Palo Alto, at Stanford Stadium. To get there, take the Embarcadero exit from Highway 101 or the Page Mill Road exit from Highway 280 and head toward the campus. The stadium is located just off El Camino Real where it is crossed by The Embarcadero. Plenty of parking is available between the stadium and the Sport Shop, on Galvez Street.

Ride 21A (Easy)

Starting on the campus, this ride takes you into the foothills above the campus along country roads, past the Arastradero Preserve to the Alpine Inn, and returns along Alpine Road.

Terrain

Easy climbing on smooth roads with adequate bike lanes or shoulders characterize the terrain of this leisurely ride through and around Portola Valley. Cyclists and equestrians are quite common on weekends, as this area is easily one of the most popular for local residents.

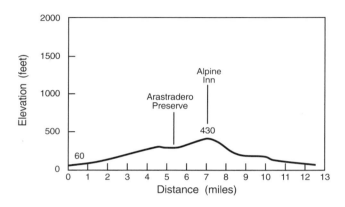

Ride 21A: Ride Details and Mile Markers

0.0 From the stadium parking lot, turn LEFT onto Galvez Street, heading into the heart of the campus, away from El Camino Real.

0.1 Turn LEFT onto East Campus Drive and follow it all the way around the campus.

1.7 Turn LEFT onto Junipero Serra Boulevard.

3.2 Turn RIGHT onto Page Mill Road.

3.3 Turn RIGHT onto Old Page Mill Road (this avoids the traffic on Page Mill Road).

4.2 Turn RIGHT to get back onto Page Mill Road.

4.5 Cross under Highway 280.

4.8 Turn RIGHT onto Arastradero Road.

5.3 Arastradero Preserve on the right side.

6.8 Turn RIGHT onto Alpine Road.

8.7 Freeway underpass.

10.0 Turn RIGHT onto Junipero Serra Boulevard.

10.5 Turn LEFT onto West Campus Drive.

12.5 Turn LEFT onto Galvez Street.

12.6 Back at the stadium.

Ride 21B (Moderate)

Ride 21B, like Ride 21A, takes you into the foothills above the campus along country roads, past the Arastradero Preserve. Continuing through the pleasant rural town of Portola Valley, the return to the campus is along Sand Hill Road and past the Stanford Linear Accelerator Center, home of some of the most advanced physics research in the world.

Terrain

Easy climbing on smooth roads with adequate bike lanes or shoulders characterize the terrain of this leisurely ride through and around Portola Valley.

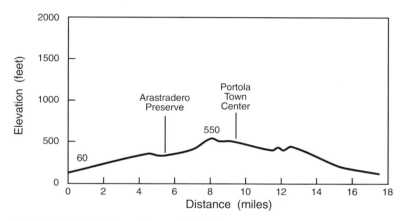

Ride 21B: Ride Details and Mile Markers

0.0 From the stadium parking lot, turn LEFT onto Galvez Street, heading into the heart of the campus, away from El Camino Real.

0.1 Turn LEFT onto East Campus Drive and follow it all the way around the campus.

1.7 Turn LEFT onto Junipero Serra Boulevard.

3.2 Turn RIGHT onto Page Mill Road.

3.3 Turn RIGHT onto Old Page Mill Road (this avoids the traffic on Page Mill Road).

4.2 Turn RIGHT to get back onto Page Mill Road.

4.5 Cross under Highway 280.

4.8 Turn RIGHT onto Arastradero Road.

5.3 Arastradero Preserve on the right side.

6.8 Turn LEFT onto Alpine Road.

8.1 Turn RIGHT onto Portola Road.

9.5 Portola Town Center on the left.

11.6 Continue STRAIGHT to stay on Sand Hill Road. (Portola Road turns to the left).

13.8 Freeway overpass.

14.9 Stanford Linear Accelerator Center (SLAC) on the right.

15.4 Turn RIGHT onto Santa Cruz Avenue.

15.5 Turn LEFT onto Junipero Serra Boulevard.

16.0 Turn LEFT onto West Campus Drive.

17.8 Turn LEFT onto Galvez Street.

17.9 Back at the stadium.

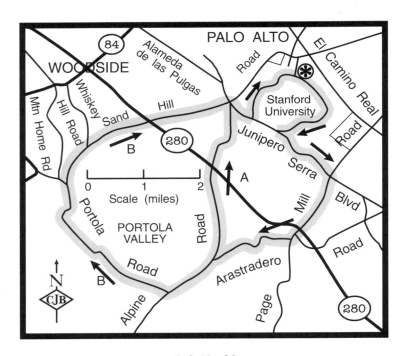

Ride No. 21

22 Cupertino
Back Door into Monte Bello Open Space Preserve

Region: *Lower Peninsula*
Total Distance: *17 miles*
Total Elevation Gain: *2300 feet*
Type of Bike: *Mountain Bike*

Ride Rating: *Difficult*
Riding Time: *3 hours*
Calories Burned: *1400*

Terrain

This ride includes a tough hill climb through beautiful parklands. The trail is steep and narrow in places, but is one of the better mountain bike rides in the Bay Area, by virtue of the sheer size of the preserve and the numerous panoramic views.

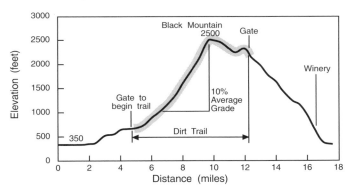

Ride Description

The Monte Bello Open Space Preserve is the largest in the Midpeninsula Regional Open Space District and encompasses over 2600 acres of marvelous scenic and natural land. It embraces the entire upper Stevens Creek watershed from the grassy slopes of Monte Bello Ridge to the brush and oak covered woodlands below. The primary access to the preserve is located on Page Mill Road, about one mile from its intersection with Skyline Blvd. However, the park may also be entered from the ends of either Stevens Canyon Road or Montebello Road.

This ride takes you up remote Stevens Canyon Road, following along Stevens Creek, and enters the Monte Bello Preserve on the Canyon Trail at the end of Stevens Canyon Road. Climbing along on a generally mild grade, the Canyon Trail takes you through the heavily wooded lower sections of the preserve. As you reach the higher elevations, grassy slopes are exposed to reveal views of the entire Stevens Creek watershed.

When you branch off the Canyon Trail to get on Indian Creek Trail, the climb becomes much steeper and you will usually have to rest periodically to catch your breath. The views get even more dramatic as you approach the communication towers at the top of Black Mountain (2500-foot elevation). From Black Mountain, you can see in all directions.

Past Black Mountain, the trail heads downhill to the intersection with Waterwheel Creek Trail, branching off to the right. This trail leads down a bit and then back up to exit the preserve on Montebello Road. Montebello Road will give you an exhilarating and fast descent back to Stevens Canyon Road, from where you started.

Starting Point

The ride starts in Cupertino on Stevens Canyon Road, just above Stevens Creek Dam, at the intersection with Montebello Road. To get there, take the Foothill Expressway and Grant Road exit off Interstate Highway 280 in Cupertino. Note that there are several exits for Foothill Expressway, but this one is the only one in Cupertino. Proceed west on Foothill Boulevard and cross Stevens Creek Boulevard, heading toward the Stevens Creek Dam and Reservoir. Foothill Boulevard then becomes Stevens Canyon Road. Continue past the dam, just beyond the intersection with Montebello Road on the right. There is a small park on the left side, at which you may park your car.

Waterwheel Creek Trail in Monte Bello Preserve

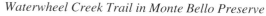

Ride Details and Mile Markers

0.0   Proceed WEST on Stevens Canyon Road, away from the dam and toward the mountains.

1.2   Bear RIGHT to stay on Stevens Canyon Road.

2.9   Redwood Gulch Road intersection on the left.

4.8   Continue STRAIGHT at the gate at the end of the road. This is the beginning of the trail which leads into the preserve.

5.0   Gravel and dirt surface begins.

5.6   Cross creek.

5.7   Trail becomes very narrow.

6.1   Bear RIGHT at the intersection with a trail on the left which goes to Saratoga Gap. Trail widens at this point.

6.4   Continue STRAIGHT at the trail intersection to stay on Canyon Trail. Trail on the left is Grizzly Flat Trail and leads to Long Ridge Open Space.

8.4   Bear RIGHT onto Indian Creek Trail, heading up toward Black Mountain. Steep uphill begins with excellent views of the Stevens Creek watershed off to the right.

8.9   Continue STRAIGHT at trail intersection on the left.

9.1   Continue STRAIGHT at second trail intersection on the left and proceed on Black Mountain Trail.

9.3   Continue STRAIGHT at Black Mountain Trail intersection on the left.

9.4   Summit at the microwave towers. Elevation — 2500 feet.

10.3   Turn RIGHT onto Waterwheel Creek Trail. (This trail descends about 200 feet and then climbs back up to Montebello Road. If you wish to avoid the climb, do not turn on Waterwheel Creek Trail, but continue straight ahead to Montebello Road.)

11.7   Continue past the barrier at the end of the trail and turn RIGHT onto Montebello Road.

16.4   Sunrise Winery on the right side.

16.8   Turn RIGHT onto Stevens Canyon Road.

16.9   Back at the start point.

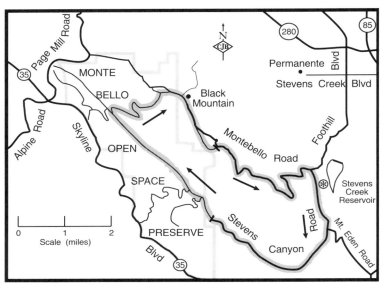

Ride No. 22

Old stables in the Arastradero Preserve

23 Palo Alto
Tour of the Arastradero Preserve

Region: *Lower Peninsula*
Total Distance: *5 miles*
Total Elevation Gain: *500 feet*
Type of Bike: *Mountain Bike*

Ride Rating: *Easy*
Riding Time: *1-2 hours*
Calories Burned: *500*

Terrain

This leisurely ride has some hilly sections, but none that are very long or climb very high. The trails are mostly wide and smooth, although there may be some ruts after recent rains.

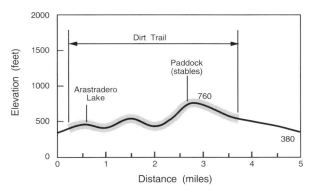

Ride Description

The Arastradero Preserve is owned by the City of Palo Alto, but is open to hikers, equestrians, joggers and cyclists, so special caution is advised. If you decide to explore the preserve on your own, be aware that some trails do not permit cyclists, so those must be avoided. The preserve consists mainly of pastureland and grassy fields with a scattering of oaks and shrubs. Along Arastradero Creek and around the lake, tall trees provide welcome shade on warm summer days.

This tour takes you through the preserve and loops you around to get a full view of the area. Leaving the preserve at the western end, you return to the starting point along rural Arastradero Road.

Starting Point

The ride starts at the parking lot for the Palo Alto Arastradero Preserve. To get there, take the Page Mill Road exit for Highway 280 and head west on Page Mill Road. After about ¼-mile, turn right onto

Arastradero Road. The parking lot for the preserve is located on Arastradero Road about ½-mile from Page Mill Road.

Ride Details and Mile Markers

0.0   From the parking lot, turn LEFT onto Arastradero Road, heading toward the Page Mill Road intersection.

0.2   Turn RIGHT to enter the preserve. Carry your bike across the barrier.

0.4   Bear RIGHT to stay on the trail at the junction with a narrow single-track trail on the left. Just after this, bear LEFT at the junction with a trail going off to the right and climb a short, steep section.

0.6   Arastradero Lake on the left side.

0.7   Turn LEFT just past the lake to get on the Corte Madera Trail (unmarked). This trail follows the creek, which will be on your left side.

1.0   Turn RIGHT onto unmarked Acorn Trail and climb up the hill.

1.2   Continue STRAIGHT at the major intersection (Meadowlark Trail) at the top of the hill to stay on Acorn Trail.

1.5   Turn RIGHT at the end of Acorn Trail a go around the chain link gate to get on the gravel service road.

1.8   Turn RIGHT at the point where a park entrance appears on the left side.

2.0   Turn RIGHT at the trail intersection to get on unmarked Meadowlark Trail.

In the Arastradero Preserve

2.3 Continue STRAIGHT at the intersection with Acorn Trail. This is the same intersection you crossed earlier.

2.7 Paddock on the right side.

2.8 Continue past the gate. This is the highest point of the ride — 750 feet.

3.3 Carry your bike across barrier and continue on the paved road.

3.7 Turn RIGHT onto Arastradero Road.

4.4 Gate into the preserve on the right side.

5.0 Turn LEFT into the parking lot to end the ride.

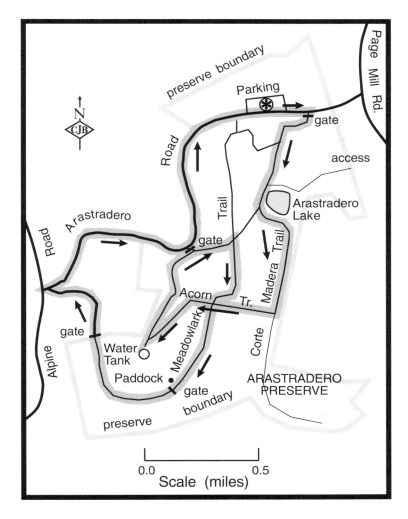

Ride No. 23

24 Portola Valley
Up Alpine Dirt Road and Down Old La Honda Road

Region: *Lower Peninsula*
Total Distance: *22 miles*
Total Elevation Gain: *2100 feet*
Type of Bike: *Mountain Bike*

Ride Rating: *Difficult*
Riding Time: *3 hours*
Calories Burned: *1100*

Terrain

A 2.5-mile stretch of unpaved Alpine Road leads up a moderately steep climb with a grade of about 8%. The remainder of the ride is on smooth country roads with some car traffic.

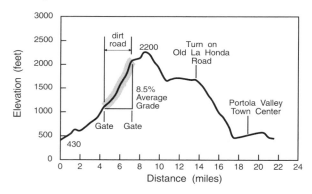

Ride Description

The Alpine Inn (fondly remembered by the locals as "Rossotti's") serves as the starting point for this ride. Alpine Road is a smooth road through beautiful Portola Valley, much favored by the many cyclists and equestrians usually found here on weekends. A relatively little-known variation of the rides that most of the locals enjoy takes you to the end of the paved portion of Alpine Road and proceeds on the old section, up a dirt fire trail leading to the top of the mountain at Page Mill Road. The road is wide and generally smooth, although ruts are common in some sections, especially after a rainfall.

At the end of the dirt road, Page Mill Road takes you to the top at Skyline Boulevard. Climbing a bit more on Skyline, there are stunning views of the Santa Clara Valley as it spreads out below you. A gentle downhill stretch of Skyline Boulevard leads to the intersection with Old La Honda Road, a delightful, little-used road which formerly served as a logging access to the forests in the area, but which today carries very little car traffic. The rapid descent on Old La Honda Road has many curves, so be ready with your brakes. At the bottom, you return to the Alpine Inn along Portola Road, passing the rustic Portola Valley Town Center on the way.

Starting Point

The ride starts in Portola Valley at the intersection of Alpine Road and Arastradero Road. To get there, take the Alpine Road exit from Interstate Highway 280 and proceed west on Alpine Road for about one mile to the intersection with Arastradero Road. Start the ride at the Alpine Inn restaurant, a favorite of local cyclists and equestrians.

Ride Details and Mile Markers

0.0 Proceed WEST on Alpine Road, away from Highway 280.

1.1 Continue STRAIGHT at the intersection with Portola Road on the right.

4.5 Turn RIGHT off the paved road to begin the dirt section of Alpine Road. You will recognize this point by the steep hill ahead of you on the paved road and by the gate off the road on the right marking the start of the dirt road.

7.1 Turn RIGHT onto Page Mill Road, just beyond the gate at the end of the dirt section.

7.8 Turn RIGHT onto Skyline Boulevard.

8.9 Vista Point on the right side.

12.8 Windy Hill Open Space Preserve on the right side.

13.7 Turn RIGHT onto Old La Honda Road and begin steep descent.

The Alpine Inn ("Rossotti's")

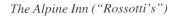

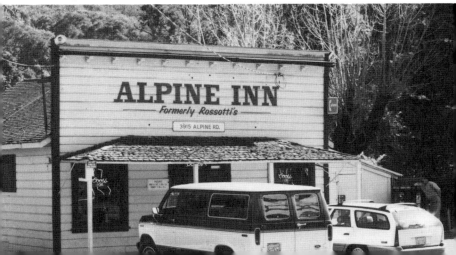

17.7 Turn RIGHT onto Portola Road at the end of Old La Honda Road.

19.1 Portola Valley Town Center on the right side.

20.4 Turn LEFT onto Alpine Road.

21.5 Back at the start point.

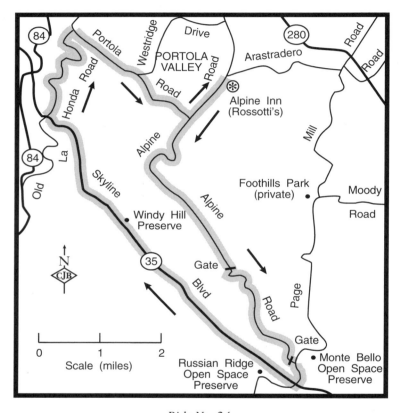

Ride No. 24

25 Palo Alto
Russian Ridge
and other Open Space Preserves

	Ride 25A	Ride 25B
Region:	Lower Peninsula	
Ride Rating:	Moderate	Moderate
Total Distance:	11 miles	7 miles
Riding Time:	2-3 hours	1-2 hours
Total Elevation Gain:	1300 feet	1200 feet
Calories Burned:	800	700
Type of Bike:	Mountain Bike	Mountain Bike

Ride Description

The Midpeninsula Regional Open Space District was established in 1972 for the purpose of acquiring and supervising undeveloped land to be used for the recreation and enjoyment by the general public. Unlike state and county parks, open space preserves are intended to remain in their primitive states, without park visitor centers, campgrounds, or developed picnic areas. Financed by tax-supplied funds, the District aspires to acquire suitable land as it becomes available for sale on the open market.

There are currently about 26 separate preserves managed by the District, encompassing over 25,000 acres, in total. Use of the preserves extends to hikers, joggers, equestrians and cyclists, although some preserves may have some individual restrictions due to the nature of the trails.

The Russian Ridge, Coal Creek, Skyline Ridge and Monte Bello Open Space Preserves are each located in the direct vicinity of the intersection of Skyline Boulevard, Page Mill Road and Alpine Road, at the top of the Santa Cruz Mountain range. Because they are at the top of the ridge, visitors are rewarded with outstanding panoramic views without the effort of making the climb all the way from the bottom.

Starting Point

Start the ride at the Russian Ridge Open Space Preserve, located above Palo Alto at the intersection of Page Mill Road, Skyline Boulevard (Highway 35), and Alpine Road. To get there, take the Page Mill Road exit from Interstate Highway 280 and head west on Page Mill Road. Proceed all the way to the top and cross Skyline Boulevard (State Highway 35) to get on Alpine Road. Just past the intersection, on the right side, is the parking lot for Russian Ridge Open Space Preserve.

Ride 25A (Moderate)

Ride 25A follows fire trails through both the Russian Ridge and the Coal Creek Preserves. Substantial climbing is required, as the trails follow the mountain ridges throughout the preserves over continuously rolling hillsides.

Terrain

Trails are generally wide fire roads. Some significant climbs are required.

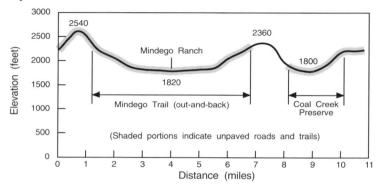

Ride 25A: Ride Details and Mile Markers

0.0 Proceed NORTH out of the parking lot on Ridge Trail, heading toward Borel Hill.

0.5 Bear RIGHT at trail junction to stay on Ridge Trail.

0.8 Bear RIGHT at the trail junction at the crest of the hill.

1.2 Turn LEFT at major trail junction to get on Mindego Trail.

1.5 Continue STRAIGHT toward Mindego Ridge at intersection with Alder Spring Trail on the right.

3.0 Turn RIGHT onto fire road at the end of the trail.

4.1 Turn AROUND and return at the end of the fire road at the Mindego Ranch. This is the preserve boundary and you must go back from this point.

5.2 Turn LEFT onto Mindego Trail, returning the way you came.

6.6 Continue STRAIGHT at the intersection with Alder Spring Trail on the left.

6.8 Continue STRAIGHT at the intersection with Ridge Trail, heading toward the road.

6.9 Leave Russian Ridge Preserve and turn LEFT onto Skyline Blvd.

7.5 Turn RIGHT onto Crazy Pete's Road and into Coal Creek Preserve. This road is very small and easy to miss.

7.8 Bear RIGHT at junction — end of paved road.

7.9 Bear RIGHT to enter Coal Creek Preserve and gate "CC04." Turn RIGHT immediately after the gate to stay on Crazy Pete's Road, heading toward Alpine Road.

8.1 Bear RIGHT at intersection with Valley View Trail on the left to stay on Crazy Pete's Road.

8.8 Cross small wooden bridge and begin uphill section on single-track trail.

8.9 Continue past the preserve barrier and turn RIGHT onto unmarked and unpaved Alpine Road. Begin climbing.

10.1 Continue past gate and turn RIGHT onto Page Mill Road.

10.7 Cross Skyline Boulevard.

10.8 End of the ride back at Russian Ridge Preserve parking lot.

On the Mindego Trail in Russian Ridge Preserve

Ride 25B (Moderate)

Ride 25B tours Skyline Ridge Open Space Preserve and the upper part of Monte Bello Open Space Preserve. Two stream crossings and narrow single-track trails in Monte Bello test your cycling skills and may get your feet wet. Since both rides begin and end at the same place, it is possible to link them together for a longer ride and a greater challenge.

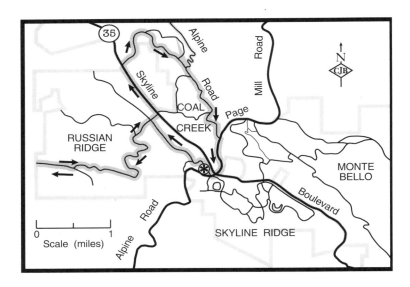

Ride No. 25A

Terrain

Expect substantial climbing on relatively wide fire roads, as well as some single track trails and two stream crossings.

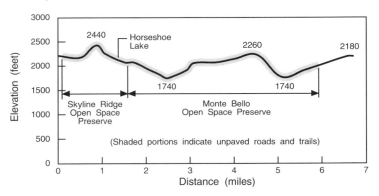

Ride 25B: Ride Details and Mile Markers

0.0 Proceed SOUTH out of the parking lot out the main road entrance and cross Alpine Road to get to trailhead into Skyline Ridge Open Space Preserve.

0.1 Cross barrier to get on the Alternate Ridge Trail toward Horseshoe Lake and Skyline Parking. This is a single-track trail which immediately proceeds downhill toward Alpine Lake.

0.2 At Alpine Lake, bear RIGHT to stay on the bicycle-only trail around the lake and then turn LEFT onto the paved road.

0.4 Unpaved trail begins just past private residences.

0.6 Turn LEFT to stay on Alternate Ridge Trail.

0.8 Crest — 2440 feet.

1.0 Continue STRAIGHT at the major trail intersection.

1.4 Horseshoe Lake on the right.

1.5 Continue past the barrier and through the equestrian parking lot. Just past the parking lot, turn LEFT onto the trail leading to the main parking lot.

1.7 Continue through the main parking lot. Just past it, turn LEFT past a barrier and cross Skyline Boulevard to reach the trailhead into Monte Bello Open Space Preserve. The gate into Monte Bello is identified by the code "MB06." Just past the gate, immediately bear LEFT and follow the trail as it runs parallel to the road.

2.1 Continue STRAIGHT toward Stevens Canyon Nature Trail at the trail junction on the left.

In the Russian Ridge Preserve

2.3 Continue STRAIGHT toward the Canyon Trail at the trail junction on the left.

2.4 Cross bridge and then cross stream.

2.5 Cross bridge and then begin steep section.

2.9 Turn LEFT on the Canyon Trail, heading toward Page Mill Road.

3.6 Continue STRAIGHT toward Los Trancos at trail junction on the left.

3.8 Turn LEFT just before the gate out of Monte Bello and stay on the trail as it follows along Page Mill Road.

4.0 Go through the main parking lot for Monte Bello Open Space Preserve to the far side of parking area and get on the continuation of the trail following parallel to the road.

4.5 Bear LEFT at the trail split to head toward Skyline Boulevard and Stevens Creek Nature Trail. The next section is narrow and descends steeply, so you may want to lower your seat for added safety.

5.4 Cross stream and begin climbing.

5.6 Turn RIGHT at the end of the trail and continue toward Skyline Ridge and Skyline Boulevard.

5.9 Cross barrier out of Monte Bello Open Space and turn RIGHT onto Skyline Boulevard.

6.6 Turn LEFT onto Alpine Road and then RIGHT into the parking lot for Russian Ridge.

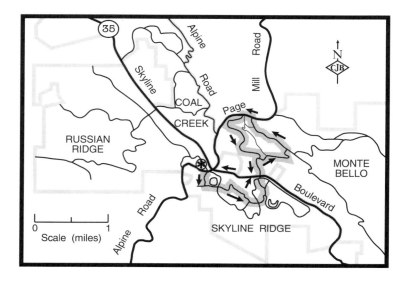

Ride No. 25B

APPENDIX

RIDES BY RATINGS

Easy Rides
(short rides, easy grades, for beginners and children)

Moderate Rides
(longer rides, some hills, not too strenuous)

Difficult Rides
(extensive rides with strenuous grades, for more experienced cyclists)

MOUNTAIN BIKE RIDES

Memorial Church at Stanford University

BICYCLE SHOPS ON THE PENINSULA

Belmont

California Sports & Cyclery
1464 El Camino Real
(415) 593-8806

Burlingame

Burlingame Cyclery
1111 Burlingame Ave.
(415) 343-8483

Daly City

Broadmoor Bicycle Shop
150 San Pedro Road
(415) 756-1120

Foster City

Beach Park Bicycles
1485 Beach Park Blvd.
(415) 349-1551

Foster City Cyclery
999B Edgewater Blvd
(415) 349-2010

Half Moon Bay

The Bicyclery
432 Main Street
(415) 726-6000

The Toy Pedaler
50 No Cabrillo Hwy #3
(415) 726-1322

Los Altos

The Bicycle Outfitter
963 Fremont Avenue
(415) 948-8092

Valley Cyclery
359 State
(415) 949-3009

Menlo Park

Menlo Velo Bicycle Shop
433 El Camino Real
(415) 327-5137

Mountain View

Action Sport
791 Castro Street
(415) 968-7723

Joselyn's Bicycles
1770 Miramonte Ave.
(415) 968-1363

Pacific Bicycle
1040 Grant Road
(415) 961-9142

Pacifica

Coastside Bicycles
1231 Linda Mar
Shopping Center
(415) 359-5920

Palo Alto

Action Sport
401 High Street
(415) 328-3180

Campus Bike Shop
551 Salvatierra
(415) 325-2945

Garner's Bike Shop
3413 Alma Street
(415) 856-2088

Midtown Bike Shop
2740 Middlefield Rd
(415) 322-7558

Palo Alto Bicycles
171 University Ave
(415) 328-7411

The Recyclery Bike Shop
1955 El Camino Real
(415) 328-8900

Valley Cyclery
3910 Middlefield Rd
(415) 493-0565

Wheelsmith
225 Hamilton Avenue
(415) 324-0510

Redwood City

Chain Reaction Bicycles
1451 El Camino Real
(415) 366-7130

Garner's Bike Shop
2755 El Camino Real
(415) 366-2453

Performance Bike Shop
2535 El Camino Real
(415) 365-9094

Redwood Cyclery
1712 El Camino Real
(415) 364-6694

Redwood Trading Post
1305 El Camino Real
(415) 363-2033

Woodside Bikeworks
777 Woodside Road
(415) 369-9848

San Bruno

The Bike Route, Inc.
488 San Mateo Ave.
(415) 873-9555

San Carlos

Steve's Sport Center
895 Laurel
(415) 593-2881

Velo Bicycle Shop
1316 El Camino Real
(415) 591-2210

San Fransisco

American Cyclery
510 Frederick Street
(415) 664-4545

Avenue Cyclery
756 Stanyan Street
(415) 387-3155

Balboa Cyclery
4049 Balboa
(415) 752-7980

Bay Area Cyclery
4537 Mission Street
(415) 585-7480

The Bike Nook
3004 Taraval
(415) 731-3838

*City Cycle of San
Francisco*
3001 Steiner Street
(415) 346-2242

Freewheel Bike Shop
1920 Hayes Street
(415) 752-9195

G& M Sales
1667 Market Street
(415) 863-2855

Golden Bike (rentals)
407 O'Farrell Street
(415) 771-8009

Lincoln Cyclery
772 Stanyan Street
(415) 221-2415

Marina Cyclery
3330 Steiner Street
(415) 929-7135

Mountain Ave. Cyclery
1269 9th Avenue
(415) 665-1394

Noe Valley Cyclery
4193 24th Street
(415) 647-0886

Nomad Cyclery
2301 Irving Street
(415) 564-3568

Nomad Cyclery
1915 Ocean Avenue
(415) 239-5004

Open Road Bicycles
1352 Irving Street
(415) 753-6272

Pacific Bicycle
1161 Sutter
(415) 928-8466

Park Cyclery
1865 Haight Street
(415) 221-3777

Presidio Bicycle Shop
5335 Geary Blvd
(415) 751-3200

San Francisco Cyclery
858 Stanyan Street
(415) 221-2412

Seal Rock Cycles
6350 Geary Blvd
(415) 387-3152

Stanyan Street Cyclery
672 Stanyan Street
(415) 221-7211

Start to Finish
633 Townsend Street
(415) 861-4004

Sutro Cyclery
4410 Cabrillo Street
(415) 386-3126

Valencia Cyclery
1077 Valencia Street
(415) 550-6600

Velo City
638 Stanyan Street
(415) 221-2453

San Mateo

Talbots Cyclery
714 South B Street
(415) 344-5994

Vince's Bicycle Shop
2176 So. El Camino
Real
(415) 341-1031

So. San Fransisco

Bicycle Shop
330 Grand Avenue
(415) 588-5111

*Windsurf/Bicycle
Warehouse*
405 So. Airport Blvd.
(415) 588-1714

CYCLING CLUBS AND ORGANIZATIONS

Auriga
221 Standish Street
Redwwod City 94062
(415) 367-6028
Long distance training.

Cal-PAL Bike Club/Team, San
Francisco
(415) 821-1411
Competititive and educational
club/team for 9-17 year olds.

Coastside Cyclist, Half Moon Bay
852 Buena Vista
Moss Beach 94038
(415) 728-5848
Recreational on-road/off-road rides.

Different Spokes
Box 14711
San Francisco 94114
(415) 282-1647
Recreational cycling for gays and
lesbians.

The Fogtown Frenzy
1454 34th Avenue
San Francisco 94122
(415) 731-FOGG
Multi-sport & social association,
cycling, hiking, cross-country skiing.

Golden Gate Cyclists, AYH
425 Divisadero, Suite 306
San Francisco 94117
(415) 863-9939
Recreational cycling, all ages and
abilities.

Menlo Park Velo Club
441 El Camino Real
Menlo Park 94025
(415) 327-5137
Racing and training.

Outdoors Unlimited
Box 0234A, UCSF
San Francisco 94143
(415) 476-2078
Co-op resources and networks for
outdoor activities.

Psychedelic Cyclists, San Mateo
County
(415) 344-7046
Racing, training, recreational rides.

*R.O.M.P. (Responsible, Organized
Mountain Pedalers),* Los Gatos
(415) 949-3137
Weekly off-road training and
recreational rides. Off-road activists.

San Francisco Bicycle Coalition
Box 22554
San Francisco 94122
Promotes the bicycle for everyday
transportation.

San Francisco Wheelmen
Box 1743
San Francisco 94101
Racing and training rides.

*Sierra Club, S.F. Bay Chapter —
Bicycling Section*
3632 Lawton #5
San Francisco 94122
(415) 665-7913
Recreational and social cycling.

Skyline Cycling Club
Box 60176,
Sunnyvale 94088
(408) 739-3995 or (408) 732-3717
Touring club, some off-road rides.

Tunitas Creek Bicycle Club,
Mid-Peninsula
Box 988
Redwood City 94064

Velo Esprit Bicycle Club
Box 50152
Palo Alto 94303
(415) 968-4177
USCF racing and training.

*Western Wheelers Bicycle Club,
Inc.,* Mid-Peninsula
Box 518
Palo Alto 94302
(415) 858-0936
Recreational touring club.

CYCLING EVENTS ON THE PENINSULA

RECREATIONAL RIDES
Le Tour de sanFRANCEcisco

  Time of year: July – Sunday nearest July 14
        Place: San Francisco
     Benefits: American Heart Association
  Information: (415) 664-BIKE

Macy's Great San Francisco Bike Adventure

  Time of year: June
        Place: San Francisco
      Sponsor: Macy's
  Information: (415) 397-3333

Sequoia Century

  Time of year: June
        Place: Southern Peninsula
      Sponsor: Western Wheelers,
  Information: Jim Evans (415) 858-0936

Banana Century

  Time of year: August
        Place: Southern Peninsula
      Sponsor: Skyline Cycling Club
  Information: Ginger Wolnik (408) 739-3995

COMPETITIVE RACING
Hangover Race, San Bruno

  Time of year: First day in January
        Place: San Bruno County Park

PERIODIC PUBLICATIONS

  California Bicyclist, San Francisco
  Published monthly, except February.
  Includes listing of organized rides and clubs.
  Available free at most bike shops.
  Information: (415) 546-7291

FAIRS AND EVENTS ON THE PENINSULA

Half Moon Bay

Chamber of Commerce
  (415) 726-5202

Harbor Day
  Time of year: late-September

Pumpkin Festival
  Time of year: October

Portuguese Festival
  Time of year: May

Chili Cook-Off
  Time of year: June

San Francisco

Visitor and Convention Center
  (415) 391-2000

Macy's Easter Flower Show
  Time of year: Late March
  Information: (415) 397-3333

Cherry Trees in Bloom
  Place: Japanese Tea Garden,
  Golden Gate Park
  Time of year: Last week of
  March
  Information: (415) 387-6787

Opening Day of the Yachting Season
  Place: San Francisco Bay
  Time of year: Last Sunday in
  April
  Information: (415) 563-6363

San Francisco Examiner Bay to Breakers Race (foot)
  Time of year: May
  Information: (415) 777-7770

Union Street Spring Festival, Arts & Crafts
  Place: Union Street
  Time of year: June
  Information: (415) 346-4446

San Francisco Fair Flower Show/ Golden Gate Festival
  Place: San Francisco County
  Fair Building, Golden Gate Park
  Time of year: August
  Information: (415) 753-7090

San Francisco Blues Festival
  Great Meadow, Fort Mason
  Time of year: September
  Information: (415) 826-6837

Fleet Week
  Place: Along the waterfront
  Time of year: October
  Information: (415) 756-6056

Los Altos

Chamber of Commerce
  (415) 948-1455

Rotary Club Art Show
  Time of year: May

Los Altos Village Association Art and Wine Festival
  Time of year: July

Palo Alto

Chamber of Commerce
  (415) 324-3121

Palo Alto Celebrates the Arts
  Time of year: Late August

Woodside

Town Hall
  (415) 851-7764

Kings Mountain Art Fair
  Place: Corner of Skyline
  Boulevard and Kings
  Mountain Road
  Time of year: Labor Day
  Weekend

POINTS OF INTEREST

State Parks

California Department of Parks and Recreation
P.O. Box 2390, Sacramento 95811
(916) 445-6477
Administration of State Park System.

Butano State Park
Cloverdale Road, Pescadero
(415) 879-0123
Hiking, camping, some bicycle trails.

Golden Gate National Recreation Area
Fort Mason, San Francisco
(415) 556-0560
Administration for Alcatraz Island, National Maritime Museum, Fort Mason Cultural Center, Sutro Baths and Cliff House, Milagra Ridge, and Sweeney Ridge.

Portola State Park
Star Route 2, La Honda
(415) 948-9098
Hiking, camping.

San Mateo Coast State Beaches
95 Kelly Avenue, Half Moon Bay
(415) 726-6238
Ranger station for administration of coastal parks and beaches.

San Mateo County Parks

c/o San Mateo County Parks and Recreation
590 Hamilton Street, Redwood City
(415) 363-4020

Coyote Point Recreation Area
San Mateo
(415) 342-0598
Bike trails, swimming beach, picnicking, marina.

Edgewood County Park
Highway 280 & Edgewood Road, Redwood City
(415) 851-7570
Hiking.

Huddart County Park
Kings Mountain Road, Woodside
(415) 851-0326
Hiking, picnicking.

Memorial Park
9500 Pescadero Road, La Honda
(415) 879-0212
Camping, hiking, picnicking, swimming in Pescadero Creek.

Pescadero Creek County Park
Wurr Road, La Honda
(415) 363-4026
Biking, hiking.

Sam McDonald Park
Pescadero Road, La Honda
Hiking, equestrian trails.

San Bruno Mountain County Park
Guadalupe Canyon Parkway, San Bruno
(415) 992-6770
Hiking.

Wunderlich County Park
Woodside Road (Highway 84), Woodside
(415) 851-7570
Hiking, equestrian trails.

Mid-Peninsula Regional Open Space District
201 San Antonio Center, Mountain View
(415) 949-5500
25 mostly undeveloped preserves for public use. Trail maps and information provided upon request.

Selected Museums

Asian Art Museum
Golden Gate Park, San Francisco
(415) 668-8921
Average Brundage collection.

Cable Car Museum, Powerhouse, and Car Barn
Washington & Mason Streets, San Francisco
(415) 474-1887
Scale models of cable cars, vintage photographs.

California Palace of the Legion of Honor
Lincoln Park, San Francisco
(415) 750-3600
European art from medieval to 20th century.

Coyote Point Museum
Coyote Point, San Mateo
Bay Area nature and ecosystems displays.

Filoli Estate
Cañada Road, Woodside
(415) 364-2880
Historic mansion and formal gardens tours, by appointment.

M.H. deYoung Memorial Museum
Golden Gate Park, San Francisco
(415) 750-3600
American art from 17th century to present.

Presidio Army Museum
Lincoln Blvd. and Funston Avenue in the Presidio, San Francisco
(415) 561-4115
Role of the military in San Francisco history.

San Francisco Maritime Natural Historic Park
Aquatic Park, San Francisco
(415) 556-3002
Photographs, ship models, relics, painting, maps.

San Francisco Museum of Modern Art
Van Ness Avenue and McAllister Street, San Francisco
(415) 863-8800
20th century abstract expressionism and photographs.

Stanford University Rodin Sculpture Garden
Lomita Drive and Roth Way, Stanford University campus

Stanford University Museum of Art
Lomita Drive, Stanford University campus
(415) 723-3469

Stanford University Art Gallery
Sierra Street, Stanford University campus
(415) 723-4177

Woodside Store
Kings Mountain Road & Tripp Road, Woodside
(415) 851-7615
Museum and stable with relics from old Woodside.

Selected Wineries

Cloudstone Vineyards
27345 Deer Springs Way
Los Altos Hills
(415) 949-0647

Congress Springs Vineyards
23600 Congress Springs Road (Highway 9), Saratoga
(408) 741-5424

Thomas Fogarty Winery
19501 Skyline Boulevard, Woodside
(415) 951-1946

Obester Winery
12341 San Mateo Road (Highway 92), Half Moon Bay
(415) 726-9463

Ridge Vineyards
17100 Montebello Road, Cupertino
(408) 867-3233

Sunrise Winery
13100 Montebello Road, Cupertino
(408) 741-1310

Miscellaneous

Pescadero Marsh Natural Preserve
Pescadero Road, Pescadero
(415) 879-0832
Hiking, birdwatching.

City of Mountain View Shoreline Park
Shoreline Boulevard, Mountain View
(415) 966-6392
Hiking, bicycling, marsh trails, golf course, sailing lake.

CALIFORNIA BICYCLE LAWS

Excerpted from the 1990 California Vehicle Code, the following descriptions explain laws which pertain to cyclists.

RIGHTS AND RESPONSIBILITIES   21200

A. Bicyclists must obey all the laws which apply to operators of motor vehicles.

B. You must never ride under the influence of alcohol or drugs.

EQUIPMENT REQUIREMENTS   21201

A. You must have operating brakes.

B. Handlebars must not be elevated above the shoulders.

C. The size of the bicycle must not be so large that the operator cannot support the bike in an upright position with at least one foot on the ground.

D. When riding at night, the bicycle must be equipped with a front light, a rear reflector, pedal reflectors, and reflectors visible from the sides, at the front of the bike.

OPERATION ON ROADWAY   21202

A. You must ride as far to the right of the roadway unless you are passing another vehicle, making a left turn, or avoiding hazardous road conditions.

B. On a one-way street, you may ride on the left side if you are as far to the left as practical.

HITCHING RIDES   21203

No person riding a bicycle is permitted to attach the bike or himself to any moving vehicle.

RIDING ON BICYCLE   21204

A. Bike must be equipped with a permanent and upright seat.

B. You may not ride as a passenger unless the bike is equipped with a separate seat. Seats for children must have adequate means of holding the child in place and for protection from moving parts on the bike.

C. Children riding as passengers must wear an ANSI-approved helmet.

BICYCLE LANES 21208

A. You must ride in designated bicycle lanes unless you are passing another vehicle in the lane, making a left turn, or avoiding hazardous obstacles.
B. You must give clear signals and operate with reasonable safety before you may leave a designated bike lane.

BICYCLE PARKING 21210

You may not leave your bicycle on a sidewalk in a way that impedes pedestrian traffic.

HAND SIGNALS 21211

It is required for bicyclists to signal turns and sudden changes in speed.

Left turn signal — left hand and arm fully extended and horizontal.

Right turn signal — left hand and arm extended to the left and the forearm pointing upward.

Slowing or stopping — the left hand and arm extended downward and the palm open-faced to the rear.

FREEWAYS 21960

You must obey signs which indicate freeways or expressways on which bicycle traffic is forbidden.

View from Higgins Purisima Road near Half Moon Bay

BICYCLING TIPS

Benefit from the experience of other by familiarizing yourself with these simple tips for better and safer cycling.

GENERAL RULES OF THE ROAD

1. Always ride on the right side of the road, with the flow of traffic, never against it. Remember that bicycles are subject to the same driving rules as cars.

2. Keep as far to the right as possible in order to allow cars plenty of room to pass. Always ride in a single file.

3. Signal when you are turning or slowing down in order to allow the rider behind you to prepare for the same and to allow cars to know what you are doing. Never act suddenly, except in an absolute emergency.

4. Never ride on freeways. This is simply too dangerous.

5. Cross railroad tracks at right angles to the tracks.

6. Cross cattleguards by getting off and walking your bike.

7. In the rain or on wet surfaces, ride slower and more cautiously then you normally would. Remember that not only are the roads wet, but your brakes are wet, as well.

8. Avoid night riding. If you absolutely must, be sure to wear highly visible clothing and carry a light.

9. Never assume that a car or another cyclist will give you the right of way. Always drive defensively.

10. Be extra cautious when passing parked cars. Watch for doors to suddenly open.

11. Avoid riding on sidewalks.

12. When making a left turn in traffic, ride assertively, but give clear signals. Be sure to wave appreciatively when another vehicle gives you clearance.

13. Always stop at red lights and stop signs. Cyclists have no special privileges.

14. Signal to trailing cyclists the presence of debris in the road (like broken glass) or potholes, either of which can be difficult for them to see.

RULES FOR OFF-ROAD BIKING

1. Know the rules for the area in which you are riding. Always stay on the trails intended for bikes. Leave the area just as you found it. Carry out your own litter and any that you find.

2. Yield to equestrians. Horses may spook when a bicycle appears suddenly.

3. Yield to hikers. Remember that they had use of the trails first.

4. Always be courteous. Nothing is worse for the sport than ill-will created by impolite actions.

5. Look ahead to anticipate encounters with others.

6. Avoid contact with trailside growth. Poison oak is very common in the South Bay and can be a very unpleasant experience.

7. Carry maps at all times. Getting lost is no fun.

TIPS ON YOUR EQUIPMENT

1. Always carry a spare tire, a tire pump, and tools.

2. Be prepared to fix your own bike. Don't count on others to do this for you.

3. Check your equipment before you go, not after you are underway. Check tire pressure, seat height, brakes, and shifters each time you ride.

4. Tire pressure is usually indicated on the side of the tire. Mountain biking in rough terrain often works better when the tires are slightly deflated. Road riding requires fully inflated tires for maximum efficiency.

5. Carry adequate water supplies. This is especially true on hot days or when you are riding in areas with no services along the way.

6. A handlebar pack or panniers are a convenience for carrying extra clothing or snacks.

7. Equip your bike with reflectors. They don't add much weight and they make it easier for others to see you.

8. Toe clips give you better riding efficiency on long rides. Mountain bikes are probably better without them, since you often need to dismount very quickly in rough terrain.

9. A rear view mirror is a useful accessory and will permit you to see approaching riders and vehicles without turning around. This is especially useful if you ride with groups and want to keep track of trailing riders.

10. A chain and lock are recommended if you anticipate leaving your bike unattended and out of view.

APPROPRIATE CLOTHING

1. A helmet is mandatory. Your head is very vulnerable without protection. Minimize the effects of a possible head injury.

2. Wear bright clothing. You want to be easily seen by vehicle drivers.

3. Lycra shorts are not necessary, but will offer more comfort on long rides. The constant rubbing of loose fitting shorts will be an annoyance and may cause a skin irritation.

4. Gloves are not necessary, but long rides can cause blisters as well as problems with blood circulation.

5. Bicycling shoes are usually only necessary for competitive riders or for those with surplus cash. Most recreational riders don't really need them. Tennis or running shoes work fine.

6. It is good to carry a lightweight windbreaker, even on warm days. High altitudes or roads along the coast are often colder than you anticipate. Furthermore, if you perspire a lot on an uphill climb, you may want to put on the windbreaker for the descent.

7. Long pants and winter gloves are usually necessary for rides in the colder months.

8. Some sort of eyewear is strongly recommended. Either cycling goggles or sunglasses will provide protection from dirt, debris, and insects as well as screen your eyes from the harmful effects of the sun's ultraviolet rays.

TECHNIQUES

1. A properly adjusted seat height will ensure you comfort and will help to avoid knee injuries, quite common for cyclists. The correct height will result in a slight bend in the knee when the leg is in its fully extended position to the lower pedal.

2. Be familiar with gear shifting so you can anticipate hill climbs and shift before necessary. It is difficult to shift when there is a lot of pressure on the pedals. Always shift while you are pedaling to ensure that the chain does not derail.

3. Be ready to brake quickly, as hazards can suddenly appear.

4. The upright position (on dropped handlebars) is usually most comfortable for the majority of road riding. Position yourself on the lower bars to reduce your wind resistance on downhill runs.

5. If your bike is equipped with toe clips, try pulling up on the pedals, as well as pushing down. This uses different muscles and can give you better efficiency for long rides.

6. When riding a mountain bike on fire trails, it is common to encounter steep downhill sections. To safely deal with these, stop and lower your seat before you descend. This lowers your center of gravity and also allows you to dismount quickly without falling to the ground. Raise your seat back to its normal position for uphill sections, to get optimum leverage on the pedals.

7. Control your speed, especially on wet road surfaces and on loose gravel of off-road trails. It is very difficult and dangerous to slow down under these conditions.

8. When riding with a group, it is both safe and polite to regroup periodically. Avoid getting spread out over great distances. It is usually best to have an experienced rider follow in the rear of the group to assist any cyclist having problems.

ABOUT THE AUTHOR

An electronics engineer by training, Conrad Boisvert, has recently begun an extended sabbatical from that career and is currently involved in other pursuits. Although born in New Jersey, his residence in northern California since 1972 has fulfilled his desire to live in a place with a variety of readily available outdoor activities. He currently resides in the Willow Glen section of San Jose.

This is his second book and follows his earlier effort entitled, *South Bay Bike Trails,* published in 1990.

Other Touring Books from Penngrove Publications

South Bay Bike Trails by Conrad J. Boisvert, 1990. $10.95. The San Francisco South Bay Area is a cyclist's paradise once you escape from the population centers and head out into the surrounding countryside. The wide variety of roads and micro-climates offer you access to an unending series of adventures. Ride along roads dominated by ranches and farmlands, through heavy redwood forests or along beautiful beaches on the Pacific Coast.

Marin County Bike Trails by Phyllis L. Neumann, 1989. $10.95. Just across the Golden Gate Bridge, Marin County combines exquisite natural beauty with sophisticated elegance to give you spectacular views, rugged cliffs, natural beaches, well-developed parks, rural farmlands, tiny hidden towns and Mt. Tamlpais. A specially designed bike route from Petaluma to the Golden Gate Bridge is also included.

Sonoma County Bike Trails by Phyllis L. Neumann, 1978, Revised Edition 1990. $9.95. Less than an hour's drive north from San Francisco brings you to tranquil country roads, gently rolling farmlands, towering redwoods, lush vineyards, local wineries, the Russian River and the Pacific coastline. A specially designed bike route from Cloverdale to Petaluma is also included.

All three books contain easy-to-challenging self-guided bike rides, complete with detailed maps, elevation profiles and photographs to help you appreciate the exceptional beauty that the San Francisco Bay Area has to offer.

Copies may be ordered directly from Penngrove Publications. Please add $1.50 for shipping and handling. California residents add 6½% sales tax (71 cents).

Penngrove Publications
50 Crest Way
Penngrove, CA 94951
(707) 795-8911